UNION J
BATTLE OF
THE BANDS

Tina Campanella is a former tabloid and magazine journalist. You can tweet her at @littlebell1982

UNION J

BATTLE OF THE BANDS

TINA CAMPANELLA

JOHN BLAKE

Published by John Blake Publishing Ltd,
3 Bramber Court, 2 Bramber Road,
London W14 9PB, England

www.johnblakepublishing.co.uk

www.facebook.com/Johnblakepub   facebook

twitter.com/johnblakepub   twitter

First published in paperback in 2013

ISBN: 978-1-78219-361-6

All rights reserved. No part of this publication may be reproduced, stored in a
retrieval system, or in any form or by any means, without the prior permission
in writing of the publisher, nor be otherwise circulated in any form of binding
or cover other than that in which it is published and without a similar
condition including this condition being imposed on the subsequent publisher.

British Library Cataloguing-in-Publication Data:

A catalogue record for this book is available from the British Library.

Design by www.envydesign.co.uk

Printed in Great Britain by CPI Group (UK) Ltd

1 3 5 7 9 10 8 6 4 2

© Text copyright Tina Campanella 2013

Papers used by Publishing are natural, recyclable products made from wood
grown in sustainable forests. The manufacturing processes conform to the
environmental regulations of the country of origin.

Every attempt has been made to contact the relevant copyright-holders,
but some were unobtainable. We would be grateful if the
appropriate people could contact us.

CONTENTS

UNION J

CHAPTER ONE

'TRIPLE J' AND GEORGE ~ SEPARATE PATHS

Louis Walsh definitely took notice as he watched the three earnest young boys bound onto the stage and yell: 'Hello, London!' Already he could already see the potential in this new group.

Met by girlish screams from the 8,000-strong audience in the capital's O2 Arena, they were a refreshing change from the hundreds of hopefuls the judges had seen that day. Shy and nervous, overconfident and bizarrely talentless, weird and wacky – the four-strong team of judges must have been tearing their hair out in frustration at what they'd had to sit through already.

With two of the lads casually dressed in white T-shirts and the other one in blue, they all shared broad smiles when Louis asked: 'So who have we got here?'

'We're Triple J,' said the confident boy in the centre to more screams of support.

UNION J AND DISTRICT 3: BATTLE OF THE BANDS

The camera panned around the audience to show just a few of the giggling girls in the crowd, all whispering and pointing. It was clear that their first impression had been a good one.

Attempting to calm the growing atmosphere, Louis asked: 'Have you got people with you here today?'

'Yeah, all our mums are backstage,' laughed a very cute second band member, setting off another round of clapping – this time from the boys' families, who were anxiously waiting with presenter Dermot O'Leary.

'They're more nervous than us, I think,' added the third and final boy in the act.

'Off you go then,' Louis said abruptly, giving them the cue for their one chance to begin.

The crowd was suddenly silent. Would these three young boys have the talent to match their looks? Might this be the last time Triple J would grace a stage before disappearing into obscurity?

From the moment they launched into song, the boys' powerful voices echoed throughout the arena as they gave the Rihanna and Calvin Harris classic 'We Found Love' every-thing they had. Moving effortlessly around the stage, their voices harmonised and soared, brimming with emotion.

Judge Gary Barlow instantly sat back in his chair – it was as if he had been metaphorically punched in the face by the wall of sound! Guest judge Rita Ora bobbed her head in time to the beat as the rumbling cheers from the audience grew and grew.

'Shine a light through an open door...'

The lyrics were spookily appropriate because everyone listening to them suddenly knew that this performance had definitely opened the door for three talented boys. Finally they finished, throwing their heads down with the effort of the last few notes. Then the trio anxiously stood back up, to be greeted by thousands of instant, screaming fans. One by one they had risen to give the boys a standing ovation.

The crowd loved them. Now all they could hope was that the judges felt the same way...

Judge and solo artist Tulisa Contostavlos was quick to voice her praise. 'This is what a boy band's about – good-looking lads,' she announced.

Louis had the excited sparkle that said 'definite potential' in his eyes, while Rita Ora enthusiastically agreed, saying: 'I think the girls will love you.'

But it was Gary Barlow who fated the boys to stardom.

'In a good boy band it's not just about looking good, you've got to sound great, too – and you really do sound great,' he told them.

Brimming with excitement, the three boys could barely believe what they were about to hear.

Tulisa: 'Yes.'

Louis: 'Yes.'

Rita: 'Yes.'

Gary: 'That's four yeses, well done!'

The arena exploded as the boys patted each other on the back in disbelief before running backstage. Throwing their arms around their mums, all three were nearly toppled over by the force of their families' affection.

And that was how the world was introduced to singing sensations Jamie Hamblett, 23, Jaymi Hensley, 22, and 19-year-old Josh Cuthbert.

Within days of the boys' audition being aired, their Twitter account, @triplejofficial, had gathered more than 60,000 followers. It was obvious that they had been a staggering success, and the boys could hardly keep up with the constant stream of tweets from fans – all wishing them luck and declaring undying love for the instant heartthrobs.

But that was just the beginning. No one could anticipate the transformation that these three boys would undergo.

By contrast, Bristol teen George Shelley was alone when he took to the stage for his *X-Factor* audition. He had no one to share a nervous smile with, or to sneak him a comforting wink if the judges were a little harsh on him. Prompted to audition by his good friend Emily Tollner, he didn't even tell his mum that he was going until the last possible moment. And so it was probably a shock to everyone who knew him when he casually walked out to take his spot in front of the judges.

Wearing a hoodie and jeans, with a guitar slung across his front, the first thing anyone noticed was his mop of perfectly constructed, immaculately messed up curls. Then he flashed his killer smile at the audience and got himself an instant fan base. With his peachy skin and fresh-faced good looks it was obvious he was going to be a firm favourite with the girls.

His grin was definitely verging on cheeky as he stood in front of the judges. Tulisa looked stern as she asked his name.

'I'm George Shelley,' he replied, without a hint of nerves.

The audience cheered and made a mental note to themselves to remember that name. If he could actually play the guitar he was clutching, and even half hold a tune, then surely this gorgeous boy was going to go far.

'How old are you?' Tulisa continued, still refusing to smile.

'I'm eighteen,' he said, prompting a wave of 'Awww's.

And the questions kept coming.

'What are you doing with yourself at the moment?' asked another judge.

George explained that he worked in a coffee shop, before he began chuckling to himself – making a few hundred more audience members fall hopelessly in love with him in the process. 'I'm going to sing "Toxic" by Britney Spears,' he added.

It was a brilliant song choice – so different to what everyone was expecting from the teen dream standing in front of them. Tulisa suddenly took notice and cracked a smile.

'Hmm… Interesting choice,' she said. 'Go for it…'

Both guitar and voice sprang to life, surprising everyone in the room. The girls in the audience were transfixed by his sweet voice and Louis looked totally overjoyed at the package of talent in front of him. Especially as he sure could play the guitar!

'I'm addicted to you…' he sang, and surely half the audience was already starting to think the same thing.

When he finished the audience moved as one to stand up and applaud the talented teen in front of them.

Louis could hardly contain his excitement as he managed: 'Great look, great vocal!'

Gary instantly agreed. 'It's a yes from me.'

'And a massive yes from me,' said Tulisa, who by now had definitely been won over.

George put his hands to his face in shock. He couldn't believe the reaction he had got. He gave the audience one last smile, along with a casual wave, before walking off stage.

All four boys had never felt so excited in all their lives. It takes guts to stand up on stage and sing in front of famous and talented stars, but for them the bold gamble had paid off. They all went back to their respective homes, buzzing with excitement. They told family and friends, and even their local newspapers about their experience. Then they had to wait for Bootcamp to begin.

UNION J AND DISTRICT 3: BATTLE OF THE BANDS

Triple J member Jamie – known as 'JJ' – excitedly told his local paper, the *Newmarket Journal*: 'I have always loved singing but never had the bottle. Singing is something I've always wanted to do and I'm grateful that I'm doing something I've always wanted to do.'

It was a sentiment that all four boys shared. Triple J and George Shelley were off to Bootcamp to begin their musical journey. There would be heartache ahead before their rebirth as the band we all love today – Union J.

But we're getting ahead of ourselves. So let's go back, before we go forward...

DID YOU KNOW?

Glamour model Bianca Gascoigne and former *Popstars* and *Pop Idol* contestant, Hayley Evetts, auditioned for the judges this season, too. Hayley made it as far as Bootcamp, but Bianca didn't get past the auditions.

CHAPTER TWO

THE UNION J BOYS ~ HUMBLE BEGINNINGS

JAMIE 'JJ' HAMBLETT

QUICK FACTS
Date of Birth: 25/3/88
Born: Newmarket, Cambridgeshire
Parents: Paul and Karin Hamblett
Siblings: Ashley, 26; Otea, 7
Grew Up: Newmarket, Suffolk
Schools: Scaltback Middle School, Soham Village College

For someone so clearly at home in one of the biggest boy bands in Britain, Jamie Hamblett had an unusual start to his singing career. But when you look at the family he comes from, it was hardly surprising that his first line of work would be working as a jockey – riding racehorses. Maybe he should be called 'GG' instead of 'JJ'!

Jamie comes from a place called Newmarket, which is at the very centre of the British horseracing world and many people in the town rely on the sport for work. His father Paul was a jockey, who later moved into training horses – work that requires getting up early every single day to muck out the horses' stables and take them for their exercise.

Not long before he himself started racing professionally, Jamie's brother Ashley had worked at one of the top stables in the family's hometown and had won a series of races. As well as Ashley and JJ's father, Paul, his uncle Martin also trained horses in Germany. And another distant cousin, Liam Heard, was a rider who helped improve horses' fitness. Horses were very much a part of JJ's life from the moment he was born, so it was no surprise when at the age of fourteen, he followed his father and brother into the horseracing industry.

With his dad's help he was apprenticed to the world-famous racehorse trainer, Sir Michael Stoute. Soon after that, he started competing as a jockey. It wasn't long before he had won his first race, and by early in his second racing season – at the age of only sixteen – he had won four races.

It seems that winning is something JJ is very good at. Despite being nearly four years younger than Ashley, by 2006 he was winning just as many races as his brother and had made a big impression on the horseracing world. During his four-year career in the saddle, he took part in 270 races and won 24 of them. Part of his success may have been down to having a dad who was ambitious. It was this ambition that would later propel him to *X Factor* fame.

Jamie said his dad was strict about the need to work hard when he was young. Whenever Jamie looked like he didn't have anything to do, his dad would say: 'Why haven't you got a ride today? Phone your agent and ask why you don't have a ride.'

Paul would tell his sons to go for a run or something, to get them out of the house. He liked the boys to be busy, and this work ethic was great preparation for the *X Factor* competition – which is tough-going!

It wasn't only his dad who used to offer him advice, though. Both Jamie and his brother would receive help and words of encouragement from racing stars like Kieren Fallon and Frankie Dettori.

By the age of sixteen Jamie was putting a lot of pressure on himself to do as well as he could. He told the *Racing Post* in 2006: 'The worst thing is when I don't live up to my expectations.'

Sir Michael Stoute described him as being a very promising young rider. 'He's getting plenty of exposure on the racetrack now and he's developed a nice position in the saddle,' he said. 'He needs to work on his strength, but he's got talent and is certainly on an upward curve. I can see the progress he's making and he's the kind of rider who could end up doing well for himself.'

It sounds just like the kind of thing that Gary or Louis might say on the *X Factor* panel, so JJ obviously had a lot of experience in being judged and taking both praise and criticism.

While racing for Sir Michael, he was given the chance to ride one of the horses owned by Her Majesty the Queen. The Queen owns several horses and many of them take part in races around the country, ridden by jockeys like JJ. About two or three times a year, Her Majesty would call in at the stables to check on her animals.

Jamie said it was a daunting experience, meeting the ruler of the country. He told the *Daily Express*: 'Once or twice a year, she would pop into the yard to check on her horses – it was so weird, seeing her.

'She sauntered in, wearing Wellington boots as if it was normal – and she walked into the horses' box that I was in at that time. She said "hello", fed the horses some grass and left. Apart from *The X Factor*, it was the most surreal moment of my life.'

As his career progressed, though he found it harder and harder to keep his weight down. If a rider is too heavy it makes it more difficult for the horses to go fast. Although Jamie wasn't overweight, he was heavier than most jockeys, many of whom are tiny compared to most people. The ones who are successful often weigh below 8 stone (51 kilos). In 2006 he weighed 7st 12lb – about two or three stone lighter than most boys in their late teens. Although his mum fed him a special diet designed to keep his weight low but his energy up, it became difficult to prevent him from becoming too heavy to make sure his horses kept on winning races.

In October 2009, he took part in his last competitive horse race. It might have been difficult for the young boy to see a different future after he was no longer able to pursue his career as a jockey, especially as this exciting job had been the sole focus of his life up until that point.

When asked in 2006 what he did in his spare time, Jamie just laughed and shrugged off the question. He didn't have time to relax – it was all about the horses.

He continued to be involved with horses by helping out at a stables run by another trainer called John Gosden. Until the day he entered the *X Factor* competition, he helped train the horses by taking them out on practice runs every morning. The riding has kept him very fit, as so many girls around the country now appreciate.

With looks that most men would die for, it was inevitable that with a body honed by such hard work and the kind of chiselled features that are made for the camera, he would try modelling and acting. But, according to his family, he has sung at home all his life. They used to hear him sing along to the radio the whole time and often thought he had more than just the ability to carry a tune. After he started carving a career in the entertainment industry, he came across the other two 'Js', Jaymi and Josh, and leapt headlong as fast as one of the horses he used to ride towards the chance to form Triple J.

JAYMI HENSLEY

QUICK FACTS
Date of Birth: 23/2/90
Born: Luton, Bedfordshire
Parents: Jackie and David Hensley
Siblings: Aaron, 17
Grew Up: Luton
Schools: Putteridge High School

As a dance teacher and choreographer for her local theatre group, Jaymi's mum Jackie had always hoped her oldest son would take up a career in the performing arts. From an early age Jaymi often joined his mum on stage with the Phoenix Players, Luton's amateur dramatics group.

The first time he took to the stage with adults was in 2001, at age eleven, when he took on one of the lead roles in the production of *Blitz!* – a musical by Lionel Bart, writer of the hit musical *Oliver!* In the same year he began attending

Luton's Putteridge High School, but despite homework and studying, he continued appearing in productions with the Phoenix Players.

At fourteen, he decided to do something incredibly brave for someone so young. He had been torn by feelings for others around him that many other people of the same age did not share. Taking them to one side one day, he gathered his family and other people close to him around him and summoned up all his courage.

'I'm gay,' he told them. It wasn't as if those who knew him best hadn't guessed, but sometimes people can react badly when so many people still find it hard to understand how anyone can be attracted to someone of the same sex. Jaymi had been worried those close to him wouldn't understand. Fortunately his family took the news really well. This allowed him to move on and concentrate on what really mattered to him – his singing career.

He later told *Heat* magazine: 'It is not a big thing for me – I came out when I was 14 to my family and friends and never had one piece of negativity.'

After leaving school at sixteen, he put his heart and soul into his plan to work in the entertainment industry and tried out for a new band called Code 5. Not only did he win a place, but the band were quickly snapped up as an exciting new boy band and were given the chance to support Irish act Westlife on one of their last series of arena gigs, called 'The Love Tour'.

As the youngest member of the five-piece act, Jaymi had only been with the four other band members for two months when he travelled up and down the country, playing some of Britain's biggest venues including Brighton, Wembley, Newcastle, Dublin and Belfast.

His bandmates included 'Ash', cousin of Antony Costa from the boy band Blue, and 'Jossy', who had both had previous stabs at boy band fame. Code 5 were brought together as a manufactured vocal harmony boy band to sing a mix of material written specially for them, as well as versions of songs by other artists, some as diverse as Lionel Ritchie.

Louis Walsh, Westlife's manager, was said to have personally chosen Code 5 as one of the support bands for the tour, but who knows if he remembered Jaymi when he performed in front of him at the auditions, five years later?

After the Westlife tour, the band continued touring before featuring in a BBC3 programme fronted by top rock record producer Tommy D, called *Singing with the Enemy*. The programme saw Code 5 having to work alongside their musical opposite, anarchic performance artists called K-Tron and The Exploding Triangles. They all had to put aside their differences and work together. The bands had just one week to dream up and record a brand new track and then perform a surprise gig in front of their die-hard fans.

Viewers watched as they struggled to live together in an intense pressure cooker of creativity and reconcile their musical differences. Despite all the attention, Code 5 didn't achieve the success they had hoped for, which left Jaymi looking for a new challenge.

After a spell at a holiday camp on the entertainment team, he returned to Luton, where the talented vocalist was able to make ends meet by teaching singing and dancing – just like his mum. At every opportunity, he did what he could to return to the stage and perform in front of a wider audience, though.

In 2010, he performed at the Maspalomas Gay Pride festival in Gran Canaria, Spain, in front of an audience of thousands. Before that he had been working as a singer, touring the clubs and bars of Britain and the resorts like those found on the beaches of Spain.

Also in 2010, he entered a competition to find singers called the Open Mic Competition. After sailing through the regional heats, he made it to the final at London's indigO2, where he sang a slowed-down version of Michael Jackson's 'Billie Jean'. It was a close-run competition and he narrowly missed out on winning by being beaten by another competitor.

Jaymi tried out for BBC1's *The Voice*, but didn't make it through to the final stages. Then in 2011, he thought his time had come when he nearly made it through to the last acts in *The X Factor*. On this occasion he was part of a band called Brooklyn, who were all from his hometown of Luton.

When the four-piece group tried out in front of Gary Barlow, Louis Walsh, Tulisa Contostavlos and Kelly Rowland, it was the first time they had performed together on stage. They had formed in January of that year and just five days later, travelled to Cardiff to audition for the ITV show. Despite hardly knowing each other and having only a few hours to rehearse, they made it through the first rounds to audition in front of a live audience of 4,000 people.

They were allowed to perform two songs: 'Forget You' by Cee Lo Green and 'In My Head' by Jason Derulo. Their audition caused some disagreements between the judges but despite this, the boys still made it through to Bootcamp. At the time, Jaymi said: 'The whole experience was just surreal. We spent twenty-four hours a day with cameras following us round. The press were everywhere and we were being driven round in big *X Factor* buses that had to go on huge detours because we were being followed by paparazzi.'

But that was as far as Jaymi and his new pals went – they were booted out before they could get to the Judges' Houses stage. The group managed to sing on a tour of schools before yet another of Jaymi's shots at the big time came to an end and he found himself looking for yet another route to success. But he certainly wasn't about to give up: this time he had got so close. He knew that fame and fortune must only be round the corner.

Within just a few months, Jaymi had met up with the other boys from Triple J and finally, he was on his way to the superstardom he was destined to achieve.

JOSHUA CUTHBERT

QUICK FACTS
Born: 28/7/92
Parents: Kathryn and Graeme Browne
Siblings: Callum, 13, and Victoria, 10
Grew Up: Winkfield, Berkshire
Schools: Cranbourne Primary, Charters Secondary School, Farnborough 6th Form College

The self-appointed frontman of the band, Joshua ('Josh') Cuthbert first found his voice when he auditioned for the part of Scrooge at Cranbourne Primary School in Winkfield, aged just eleven.

Mum Kathryn later recalled the event for the *Bracknell News*, saying: 'I had no idea he had a voice – we were blown away by him singing. We got him straight into Stagecoach in Bracknell, who told him to audition for *Chitty Chitty Bang Bang*.'

Less than a year later he was performing in the magical car musical at the London Palladium as 'George', alongside Jason Donovan, Christopher Biggins and the late Stephen Gately of Boyzone, who played the child catcher. He had the role for an exhausting nine months!

Between 2003 and 2008, he attended Charters School in Ascot, Berkshire, near the Windsor home of HM the Queen. The school has a track record for producing some great entertainers, despite being a specialist sports and science college. Among those who have been a student is Chesney Hawkes, known for his number one hit, 'The One And Only'.

As well as being a great singer and performer, Josh was also a fab footballer and played for Ascot United's junior team. Martyn Parker, co-headteacher of Charters School, remembers him as someone who would liven up a classroom with his sense of humour.

Mr Parker has since told the *Bracknell Forest Standard*: 'Josh is well-remembered by staff and some pupils at Charters as a real character, who brought a smile to the face, could be a bit cheeky, but had a sparkle about him.'

In 2006, he joined his first band, Westend Boys – a five-piece that included his eventual manager, Blair Dreelan. (Blair also tried out as an *X Factor* contestant but wasn't so successful.)

Eagle-eyed *X Factor* fans might have recognised Josh when he appeared in Triple J because as part of Westend Boys, he attempted to get into the 2007 *X Factor* finals. The group made it to Bootcamp, where they were sadly axed. Josh admits it may have cramped his style, having his mum chaperone him everywhere because he was still so young. He was only fifteen! The following year the band split up and went their separate ways.

Between 2008 and 2010, he attended Farnborough Sixth Form College but after tasting musical success he was determined to keep trying to break into the notoriously tough industry. In the year before he finished college, Josh was hard at work trying to find his next musical project.

He got together with another group of friends to form new band Boulevard. With him in the Ireland-based band were singers Ryan Davis and Andy Rice, along with Alistar Jay, who eventually joined Eli Prime – a band that later impressed the judges at the Manchester auditions of *X Factor* 2012.

By March 2011, Josh was supporting Boyzone on tour with Boulevard at a small series of gigs in Ireland, including the INEC, Kilarney, The Royal Theatre, Castlebar, and Belfast's Odyssey. They also supported *X Factor* legends Jedward in Dundalk and at the time were being tipped as Boyzone's replacements.

Singer Andy Rice told the *Dundalk Argus* at the time: 'The band are currently working on an album. We've already recorded a few tracks so far and over the next couple of months, we hope to finish it off and then finalise a deal with a label.'

But things didn't quite work out quite the way they'd all hoped, and Josh ended up spending five months selling mobile phones in Wokingham for the telecoms giant '3'. Later, he got a job as a new business executive for a computer firm called Tectrade. On his LinkedIn page, Josh described his skills as: 'Communicational skills, Confidence, Customer Interaction, Building Relationships'.

Eventually though, he got back in touch with his old bandmate Blair Dreelan, who in the meantime had himself appeared on *The X Factor*, hitting the headlines when his girlfriend left him for 2010 winner Matt Cardle.

It was Blair who took Josh, JJ and Jaymi to *The X Factor* as Triple J, before they were disbanded and reformed as the band we now know and love: Union J.

GEORGE PAUL SHELLEY

QUICK FACTS
Date of Birth: 27/07/93
Born: Bristol
Parents: Toni Harris and Dominic Shelley
Siblings: Tom, 29; Will, 23; Harriet, 16
Grew up: Clevedon, Somerset
Schools: Yeo Moor Primary, King Alfred Comprehensive, Weston College

George Shelley comes from a very musical family. His mum Toni plays the guitar and used to perform in pubs near their home in North Somerset. When he was younger, his granddad Dave was in a rock and roll band. These days the retired policeman, now 75, is keeping up the family's musical tradition by entertaining the residents with his accordion in retirement homes! George's brother Tom is a drummer whose band has just recorded their first single in Australia and his uncle John is also a singer and songwriter.

Coming from such a talented family, George was destined to follow in their footsteps. When he was just a toddler, his mum encouraged George's budding musical ability by giving him empty washing-up bottles filled with a small amount of rice – a maraca! George was fascinated and was quickly shaking the maracas along in time to his favourite songs, while his family sang along. They must have been like the modern equivalent of music legends The Osmond Family or The Jackson Five.

Toni took pictures of her son pretending to play the drums, with a huge grin on his face. George would use a wooden spoon to bang pots and pans, copying the stars he saw on TV. His talented mum was also a nurse and named George after an elderly patient she used to care for when she was working.

When he was three, George's parents split up and George, his two brothers Tom and William and his sister Harriet went to live with his mum. He continued to be fascinated by music and soon after he became a teenager his granddad Dave 'busker' Harris bought him his first guitar. Almost immediately, he had mastered the instrument and at just fourteen, took to the stage at the Priddy Folk Festival, in a village near to his family's home.

His mum Toni, who has also taught aerobics, told his college website: 'George sang as soon as he could talk and is able to harmonise perfectly. He's never had a guitar lesson in his life but he's got a natural ability.'

And speaking to the *Weston-Super-Mare People*, she said: 'We have a musical family and his granddad Dave was a real rock and roller.

'George, even as a young boy, always wanted to join in and used to pretend he was playing on the drums, using a saucepan and a wooden spoon. We also used to make instruments by filling up washing up bottles with rice. He has always loved singing, dancing and playing instruments and enjoyed drama and being in plays.'

She added: 'He has always been the sort of person who could pick up an instrument and play it – a talent he got from his granddad.'

While at school, George wasn't sure if he could make it as

a full-time musician. He was wise enough to know that it was difficult to make a living out of music when there are so many wannabe stars out there to compete with. So although he kept his musical dreams alive, he sensibly worked hard on his schoolwork, too. As well as music, he had always had a passion for art. He decided that he would study graphic design, so he could become a designer and travel abroad.

At Weston College he was considered an outstanding student and won distinctions in all his subjects, completing an Extended BTEC in Graphic Design. As part of the course, he got to travel to New York. He loved it so much out there that he ended up wondering if a career in graphic design in America was what he really wanted to do. He applied to study at a higher level and ended up winning a place on a foundation course at the prestigious Bath University.

Concerned as to whether he could live up to the musical standard set by so many members of his family, he kept his bid for stardom quiet while growing up. But his musical past kept nagging away at him and he could never dismiss the lingering desire to sing on stage. He confided in his friend Emily Tollner, who suggested that he should audition for *X Factor*.

Having made it through to the later stages of the auditions, George felt he had no choice but to consider taking a year out between school and college to see how far he could get. If this was his one chance, then he would give it all he had but it hadn't been easy for him at home in the run-up to entering the competition.

His mum Toni also had to fight her own battle after she suffered a stroke in March 2011. George and the family lived through a terrifying few hours after she was rushed to hospital, where she was initially diagnosed with a severe migraine and sent home. Despite being released, her symptoms continued and the normally fit and active mum knew something wasn't right.

Toni actually experienced a bleed in her brain, which continued when she was sent home and left her with loss of feeling on her left side. She has also had recent extensive surgery on both wrists for a condition known as carpal tunnel syndrome and has been unable to find work since. She said: 'It isn't very easy given my medical history, but I am feeling much better and it's wonderful to be part of this experience with George.'

With his mum unable to work, George has also needed to make ends meet to help in his goal to achieve fame. So he found a part-time job as a barista at Costa Coffee.

Despite the scares at home and his fears over whether it was the right thing to do, George listened to his friend Emily and went after his goal of achieving singing success. Unlike his bandmates, he turned up at the *X Factor* auditions on his own and immediately impressed the judges with his good looks, boyish charm and striking voice. With a clear musical talent too, it was not long before he was singled out and added to the lineup of one of the UK's hottest new young acts.

CHAPTER THREE

BOOTCAMP ~ FATE LENDS A HAND

Both Triple J and George Shelley had made it through to Bootcamp, but they had a long way to go yet. They'd had time to calm down from the initial excitement of their successful audition, and all their friends and family had told them over and over that they were so talented – they really believed they could do it. This was their big chance...

But as they travelled to Liverpool for the intense three days of Bootcamp, their nerves had all started up again. Only 25 acts would go through to the Judges' Houses and when they arrived at the Echo Arena, the boys could see that it would be an epic competition.

The room was full – with 211 acts, to be exact, and the judges would have to be super-harsh when they made their final cuts. One small slip-up and they would be out.

The tension was unbelievable. Hardly anyone ate or drank

anything; they were all so nervous. The waiting room was a cacophony of voices, all singing different songs at the same time.

The boys were all relieved when they survived the shocking first cut, which saw 70 acts eliminated from the competition in a new twist for the *X Factor* contestants. Those acts weren't even given the chance to sing again before they were axed. For them, their dreams were over – for that year, anyway. Plenty of people audition for the show year after year, hoping they will have improved enough to finally make it.

The rest of the singers were put into groups and had to take part in a nervewracking sing-off.

As the three days passed, the number of acts slowly dwindled. Many went home and had to be comforted by their friends and family.

George Shelley had met Triple J during these exciting days and had instantly liked Josh, JJ and Jaymi. They were all of a similar age, and bonded over their shared nerves. But Triple J were sad when they found out that George didn't make it through Bootcamp.

He left Liverpool and went home, wishing his new friends in Triple J all the best and trying to figure out how he would ever get used to normal life again. Meanwhile, Triple J were still going strong, but now the judges had a problem. They'd found it really difficult to whittle down the acts, and now they were well and truly stuck: there was one spot left and two bands who desperately wanted to fill it.

Both were talented and good-looking groups of guys and it would be hard to choose between them.

They were GMD3 and Triple J.

The two hopeful bands would have to go head to head in front of the judges and they needed to sing their hearts out for the final spot.

Standing on stage, Triple J looked over at their rivals. They were handsome lads and they could certainly sing – they'd heard them practising so they knew they would be stiff competition.

Gary looked at them all and explained the situation.

'Okay, guys, the only way of settling this is to battle it out,' he said. 'We want to hear you sing again.'

Each band took a minute to decide what they would perform. They all huddled together, whispering secretively. Sipping water, Josh told the other Triple J boys: 'We've just got to not make a mistake.'

It was true, but the boys were so nervous, it would be difficult not to let everything overwhelm them.

'Triple J, can you go first?' asked Gary, kindly. Nodding in reply, the boys took a few deep breaths and began.

Their words echoed hauntingly around the stage. Harmonising to 'Yeah' by Chris Brown, the GMD3 boys bobbed their heads to the sound of their rivals' voices. It was clean and in time, and the boys had done themselves proud.

The judges watched intently as they performed with no backing track. Even GMD3 looked nervous, which the Triple J boys took to be a good sign.

'Okay, guys,' Gary said to GMD3. 'Are you ready?'

This was it – this was what it had come down to. The next few minutes would decide whether Triple J would go on to be mentored at the Judges' Houses – or whether they would be going home. They just had to hope that whatever the GMD3 boys sang, it wasn't as good as what they'd just offered up to the judges. But sadly, it was…

Singing 'Bless the Broken Road', the performance was almost faultless. They sounded much less nervous than Triple J, and the boys wished that they'd had the chance to go second. It had given Greg, Mickey and Dan time to compose themselves, with the result being a beautiful performance.

Triple J looked devastated but the judges hadn't immediately made up their minds, and instead they whispered to each other, deep in concentration.

All the boys could do now was wait.

'It's very close, there's not much between them,' said Gary, knitting his brow in concentration.

'This is tough, they both did so good,' said former Pussycat Doll and fellow judge Nicole Scherzinger.

On stage, Triple J looked close to tears, desperately hoping for the wait to end. It was torture for all the boys, who had worked so hard to get to that stage. Finally, Gary spoke. It was time to put everyone out of their misery.

'Okay, guys, you've been neck and neck throughout this competition and I'm sorry it's come down to this,' he said, 'but we've got to pick one of you right now.'

He paused while both the bands made silent prayers.

'The act taking the last place at the Judges' Houses is… GMD3.'

It was all over for Triple J.

The boys were gutted.

JJ courageously said thank you to the judges, before throwing his arms around Mickey from GMD3.

Backstage, the boys wiped the tears from their eyes and once more embraced.

'We're not going to walk away downhearted,' they said after composing themselves. 'We've got this far, we've got to keep our heads high and carry on.'

Then they went home, where their families tried their best to console them.

Soon after, Louis' bands were all set to fly to Las Vegas for the next stage of the competition – the Judges' Houses. Rough Copy, MK1, GMD3, Mitsotu, Poisonous Twins and Duke all had their bags packed and were ready to go. But before they could leave, Rough Copy received some devastating news: one of the band members had a visa application being considered by the UK Border Agency and so he couldn't leave the country in case he wasn't allowed back in.

The producers were so excited about them as a band, but they found out about the potentially difficult situation just as they were organising flights for everyone. The judges had no choice but to axe Rough Copy from the competition. And that left space for one act to be recalled to *The X Factor* – but who would it be?

Louis had a lot of thinking to do. There were two bands that he was considering taking to the next stage in their place – Times Red and Triple J. But there wasn't enough time to decide between them so they were both invited along to the Judges' Houses round.

Triple J couldn't believe their ears when they heard the news. They had gone back to their old lives and old jobs, and were trying hard to move on, but now they were back in *The X Factor*! With one more chance to show they were worthy of the public's adoration, they packed their suitcases in a hurry to leave.

But Louis had one more surprise up his sleeve: he hadn't been able to stop thinking about another of the acts that the judges had axed. And he had an idea that wouldn't go away. He picked up the phone and dialled one more number…

George Shelley was at home in Bristol when the phone rang. As the caller started to speak he couldn't believe who he was talking to. Louis Walsh. *X Factor* Judge. Boy Band King.

'Yes, yes, of course,' he mumbled. And then put the phone down. Had that conversation been real? Did Louis Walsh really just say what he thought he'd said?

George was back in *The X Factor*! He was going to join his new friends, Triple J, to make the band a fab foursome. And they would have a new name.

Union J was born.

DID YOU KNOW?

Josh's nan spent over £800 on tickets to see him in *Chitty Chitty Bang Bang* – she went every week!

Let's take a look at who made it through Bootcamp...

MENTOR: NICOLE SCHERZINGER (BOYS)

JAHMENE DOUGLAS

Fact: Schoolfriends of the shy Swindon supermarket worker used to pay him in sweets to sing.

NATHAN FAGAN-GAYLE

Fact: Nathan had two top 40 singles before joining *The X Factor* – under the guise of 'StarBoy Nathan'.

JAKE QUICKENDEN

Fact: A lifeguard from Scunthorpe, Jake hoped to win so that he could pay his mum back the cash he owed her.

ADAM BURRIDGE

Fact: An admin worker from Middlesex, Adam dreamt of playing at Glastonbury.

JAMES ARTHUR
Fact: James ran away from home when he was young and has always said music is his coping mechanism.

RYLAN CLARK
Fact: An Essex model, Rylan's dream is to release a dance album.

MENTOR: TULISA CONTOSTAVLOS (GIRLS)

JADE ELLIS
Fact: A London bike mechanic, this single mum hoped to win to provide a good life for her daughter.

AMY MOTTRAM
Fact: Student Amy has been nicknamed the 'Essex Adele' because of her big voice.

LUCY SPRAGGAN
Fact: The Sheffield portrait-seller bravely performed her own song at the first audition.

LEANNE ROBINSON
Fact: A sales assistant in London, Leanne prided herself on having no gimmick about her – just a fab voice.

ELLA HENDERSON
Fact: Ella overwhelmed the judges, but couldn't believe she'd got through Bootcamp.

JADE COLLINS

Fact: The Belfast student enlisted her mum's help to make her stage outfits.

MENTOR: LOUIS WALSH (GROUPS)

MITSOTU (HOLLY COOPER, JAMES COLLINS AND JIMMY ESSEX)

Fact: The North London trio said they were shocked at how emotional it was on the show – and by the lack of sleep!

DUKE (MARKO PANDAZIS, EDWARD TRAVERS AND FLYNN STRONACH)

Fact: The beatboxers from Gloucestershire got a massive 2,000 new Twitter followers in the two hours after their first audition.

MK1 (CHARLIE, REAL NAME, LOTTE RUNDLE AND SIMEON DIXON)

Fact: The London dubstep group dropped their third member after the judges said he looked like an accountant!

POISONOUS TWINS (STEPHANIE MCMICHAEL AND SOPHIE HOUGHTON)

Fact: This was Liverpool born Steph's second try at fame – after being first out of 2008's *Big Brother*.

TIMES RED (STAZ NAIR, SCOTT RITCHIE, LUKE WHITE)

Fact: Geri Halliwell was particularly taken by the sexy Times Red trio.

And of course, our boys: Union J and District 3.

MENTOR: GARY BARLOW (OVER 28S)

BRAD SHACKLETON
Fact: A London motivational speaker, Brad's dream was to work with Gary Barlow.

MELANIE MASSON
Fact: The Glaswegian full-time mum-of-two belted out Janis Joplin's 'Cry Baby' at her audition.

CHRISTOPHER MALONEY
Fact: The Liverpool customer services adviser deliberated for five years before entering *The X Factor*.

CAROLYNNE POOLE
Fact: A casino singer from Huddersfield, Carolynne got as far as the *X Factor* Judges' Houses in the previous year.

KYE SONES
Fact: A London chimney sweep, Kye used to be in electro-pop band, Diagram Of The Heart.

NICOLA-MARIE BLOOR
Fact: The Derbyshire lass had been an Amy Winehouse and Lady Gaga tribute act before she went to auditions.

CHAPTER FOUR

JUDGES' HOUSES ~
WHAT HAPPENS
IN VEGAS

Landing in Las Vegas, it must have seemed like a whole new world for the Union J boys. The acts that perform here are mega-stars – singers who pack out casino stages, night after night. Mariah Carey, Elvis Presley, Elton John, Barbra Streisand... The echo of every music legend's voice has reverberated around this very city.

Tulisa had taken the girls to St Lucia with Tinie Tempah, while Nicole jetted the boys to Dubai with R&B star Ne-Yo. Gary and the Over-28s remained in England, travelling to Boughton House in Northamptonshire, where they were joined by a surprise guest: Cheryl Cole. Her appearance was so top-secret that she had to hide under a tablecloth while the acts performed!

But our two favourite bands were in Vegas for one reason only – to prove to Louis Walsh and his sidekick Sharon

Osbourne that they should go through to the live stages. It was a dramatic backdrop for the next stage of the battle.

Sitting in a plush hotel, more decadently decorated than their wildest dreams, Union J spoke from the heart about their experience so far.

'We weren't even meant to be here, originally,' mused Jaymi. 'We've been given such a lifeline.'

Josh was keen to include George in their new band, and said: 'George has only been with us for three or four days so it's been a bit of a rollercoaster, to say the least.'

George certainly looked at ease with the boys, who could hardly keep still with excitement.

Reclining in his leather seat, JJ said: 'We feel like brothers, he fits like a missing puzzle piece. We feel ten times stronger than ever we were as a three.'

Having been together for such a short period of time, the boys must have been nervous about singing for Louis and Sharon. But as night fell over Vegas, it was time for the foursome's first performance together. They walked down a huge cast-iron staircase onto an amazing roof deck, which overlooked the famous Vegas strip. Millions of coloured lights twinkled and flickered behind them.

The walk must have felt as if it took hours, but in just a few seconds they were sat facing the judges.

Breaking the tense silence, Louis spoke first. 'What would it mean to you guys to get through to the live shows?' he asked.

'It would mean everything, it's what we want so much,' said Josh. 'Going back to our normal jobs after Bootcamp was horrible because reality hit us and it's something we've dreamed of.'

Nervously shuffling their feet, they tried to keep the fear from their faces as Louis said, simply: 'Off you go…'

George started strumming on his guitar and Josh began to sing 'Call Me Maybe', the song they'd performed as Triple J at the auditions. One by one George, Jaymi and JJ joined in and together their confidence grew. On their own they could sing, there was no doubt about that, but together they were transformed into a professional slick group, brimming with talent.

They may have been a little rough around the edges, but this was the real start of their journey and it had a huge impact on their growing fan base.

Sharon, wearing a white jacket, grinned at Louis. She nodded her head as Union J finished their song.

Waiting for their reaction, the boys must have been disappointed when Louis signalled for them to leave, saying: 'Thank you very much.'

Silently they trooped back to where Dermot O'Leary was waiting for them. 'How did it go?' he asked, gently.

It was, they agreed, very emotional.

Under the stars, Louis and Sharon discussed their performance. 'A couple of them have picked up really novice bad habits,' said Sharon, gravely. However, Louis came to their defence, saying: 'But with a bit of work they could be fantastic.'

There was nothing the boys could do now but wait for the verdict.

DID YOU KNOW?

Jaymi has a whopping seventeen tattoos and claims that some of them are very tricky to find...

The next day the sky was a brilliant blue. The sun shone on the handsome boys as they stood on the same deck on which they had performed the night before. They were dressed casually, but there was nothing casual about what was about to happen. At last they would find out if all the heartache had been worth it – would they be in the final twelve? Would they grace the *X Factor* stage in the live shows?

Josh clutched his hands together as if he was praying, as Jaymi said: 'We've already had one no and we don't want to go home devastated again – we've waited so long for this. Louis brought us back because he saw a spark in us and then to come here and blow it – we'd be devastated.'

Josh tried to say that he didn't want to let his family and friends down, but the tears falling down his cheeks were so heartfelt that no one was listening to the words coming out of his mouth – those tears spoke volumes enough.

Seeing his bandmate cry affected JJ deeply, and the pair of them broke down and had a little weep together. They're such a close bunch that it was bound to happen. George tried to comfort them so that everyone could compose themselves for the verdict, which was merely moments away.

Biting their nails, they listened as Louis, sporting sunglasses, began to reveal his decision.

'Guys, we loved your first audition, we saw great potential and in the sing-off that's when you showed a little bit of spark.'

The boys nodded and tried to take deep breaths to calm themselves down.

'George, putting you in, it was a bit of a gamble. I think you fitted in very well with the band but there's an awful lot of work to be done and we haven't got months, guys.'

It wasn't sounding very positive and Josh, who had just finished wiping his tears away, began to sob once more.

'The problem is, boys, there are other boy bands in this

competition who have the edge on this group because they've been together longer. I thought long and hard about it, guys. We're in Vegas and I'm not a gambling man...'

The moment was coming and it was all too much for the boys. They'd been through such an emotional time; they didn't know what to think or feel anymore. As they all began to weep, they could hardly hear Louis.

'...until today. You're through!'

The boys were stunned and for a split second they let it all sink in. They were in! They would sing live on the *X Factor* stage, seen and heard by millions of potential fans. All they could do was jump up and down and hug each other, yelling: 'We're going to the finals!'

'Don't let me down,' warned Louis.

DID YOU KNOW?

When Union J were announced as one of Louis' final three, One Direction's Louis Tomlinson went crazy with excitement, tweeting: 'Yeyyyyy I really like Union J!!'

Here are the final thirteen lucky acts who made it through to the first live show:

James Arthur
Rylan Clark
Jahmene Douglas
Jade Ellis
Ella Henderson
Lucy Spraggan
Christopher Maloney (wildcard)
Melanie Masson
Carolynne Poole

UNION J AND DISTRICT 3: BATTLE OF THE BANDS

Kye Sones
District 3
MK1
Union J

CHAPTER FIVE

UNION J
GO LIVE!

WEEK ONE ~ HEROES
6/7 October 2012

What Union J sang: 'Don't Stop Me Now' – Queen

What the judges said:
Tulisa: 'What was important was missing – if you get through this week, I need to hear vocals.'
Gary: 'You're a good band, but Louis, you've destroyed their night.'
Nicole: 'Well done for performing for the first time as a group.'
Louis: 'We'll get it right next week.'

The sun was shining on a beautiful October day as the black

cab drew up at the Corinthia Hotel in London – a 294-room palace of a hotel, just minutes away from Trafalgar Square.

As the now four members of Union J got out and looked at the grand entrance, their faces lit up. If they were lucky, this could be their home for the next few months.

'This is a lot nicer than my house at home,' said Josh, staring in amazement.

'I bet the Queen lives here,' added JJ, walking up the huge steps to where a smartly dressed doorman was waiting to let them in.

'Welcome to the Corinthia Hotel,' said a smiling receptionist as she handed over the keys to the suite. She and the rest of the smart hotel's staff would have a huge job on their hands – keeping out the hordes of *X Factor* fans who would surely soon arrive, hoping to catch a glimpse of their latest idols.

'This is still like a dream,' said Josh, as they stepped into the swanky lift. Opening the door to their suite, the boys' eyes widened still further: it was huge! Plush purple and gold cushions lay across the enormous bed – there was a giant TV screen and even a lounge. It must have felt like being given the keys to their own brand new flat, complete with maid service and room service.

'Shotgun!' yelled George, leaping onto the bed and claiming it as his own.

'Oh no!' the others groaned, 'You're not shotgunning the bed!'

But there was plenty of room for everyone in the beautiful suite. And anyway, once they'd unpacked they had little time for exploring.

They were taken for vocal coaching before heading off to have choreography lessons with legendary dancer and choreographer Brian Friedman. He has worked with stars like Britney Spears and Salt-n-Pepa, and even organised the moves in the film *Charlie's Angels*.

In the huge dance studio, Brian took them through some steps before giving the boys some advice. 'You have to be the heartbeat of the party,' he told them. 'You have to sell that this is a united group. Union is part of your name, so what I need more of from you is interaction with each other.'

He would be responsible for taking the boys' raw talent and honing them into stars.

With their singing and dancing being taken care of, it was then time for the stylists and hairdressers to work on their look. The boys couldn't believe how much pampering and preening they had to go through. They had their eyebrows plucked, their hair cut and styled and they even went for facials.

'It was literally like a star treatment, that we're not really used to,' said George.

Next they were whisked to the famous *This Morning* studios, to reveal their feelings on their new band to the nation. George told the presenter that he'd always hoped to be put into a band, so he had got his wish!

'I came into *X Factor* hoping to be put into a group scenario,' he said. 'Especially after my first audition, I felt like I need something around me.'

Sitting beside him on the sofa, JJ, Josh and Jaymi grinned, showing how happy they were to have George on board.

Jaymi admitted that it had been a rollercoaster of a journey so far, and he was just happy to be back with a second chance. 'We auditioned as a three-piece and we didn't make it through Bootcamp,' he said. 'Then Louis rang the house and said, "Guys, I've had a problem with one of the groups' visas so we're going to offer you a place at Judges' Houses – plus we're going to add George.'''

The boys were obviously happy with their new line-up. They were now one step close to becoming a superband…

Union J had just over a month to get to know each other properly and rehearse for the live shows. They had to make their acts as slick as their fellow groups, MK1 and GMD3, who had both been together for years and knew each other like brothers.

Speaking about George, Jaymi told the *This Morning* viewers: 'We met at Bootcamp and bonded really, really strongly and when we came out of the competition we stayed in contact. He has just fitted in straight away and we love having him.'

DID YOU KNOW?

When Triple J met George at the auditions, they had been thinking of asking him to join their band anyway so it was perfect when Louis became their musical matchmaker!

That week they also spilled the beans about some of the difficulties they faced in Vegas – with one of the other bands. According to the boys, one group were using some dirty tactics in Sin City. And surprisingly, it was the only girl band in the group – Poisonous Twins – who they described as an absolute nightmare.

'They would just speculate,' George explained to Heatworld.com. 'They were just poisonous. All the way through the Judges' Houses they were speculating about what was going on.'

At first, they had got on with the two girls – before their

gossiping began to drive them nuts. 'When we got there they were saying, "Oh, we just overhead someone saying that they're going to split the boy bands up and stuff."'

Josh said it was a dirty tactic, while sensitive Jaymi seemed upset by it all. 'It's sad because we thought they were quite close with us. When we got there, they were really nice to us.'

Apparently the duo even told Union J that they'd heard rumours that the show's producers were going to kick George out of the group – after he'd only just joined them.

'They were saying this just before we were about to go on and sing,' said Jaymi.

Luckily for the confused boys, Poisonous Twins didn't make it through to the first live show. And the rest of the contestants were getting on so well they felt like one big happy family.

All week they worked hard on their performance, getting themselves ready for the first live show. But they did take time out to eat together, where they constantly messed around, throwing bits of food at one another and teasing each other.

They stopped practising one night to head over to the famous celebrity club Whisky Mist, where they were showered with female attention. Joined by Jade Ellis and Lucy Spraggan, MK1, Carolynne Poole, Kye Sones and Rylan Clark, the boys soaked up the celebrity lifestyle before the live shows had even begun. But though they had a few drinks, they didn't overdo it. It was just a chance for the boys to have one final night off before the fight of their lives began.

On the day of the live show, the boys filmed a short segment to be aired that night, where they spoke about how they were coping, spending so much time together. 'We're even bathing together,' joked JJ, much to the amusement of the others.

It was clear the boys were really looking forward to the first live show. 'We're really excited to get the chance to sing in front of Olympic stars,' said Josh. But there was one particular athlete they couldn't wait to meet.

'Laura Trott's going to be in the audience,' said JJ.

'She's really hot,' said Josh. 'Hot to Trott!'

'Nooo!' cringed the others, putting their heads in their hands and groaning at the bad pun.

'That's really cringy,' said George, giggling.

DID YOU KNOW?

Louis Walsh had a hair transplant before the latest *X Factor* series. No wonder his barnet was looking so lustrous!

That night, hearing their own voices on the pre-recorded snippet from backstage, the boys prepared to take their first steps onto the *X Factor*'s live stage. And they had a surprise before the show: One Direction were there to give them some advice.

The boys were definitely starstruck to see their heroes, and when they were all mingling, it was hard to tell them apart. They looked like one big superband!

'Just have fun,' the established singing sensations told the next big things. 'Literally, just go out there and have fun.'

One Direction had been in their shoes at that first *X Factor* live show two years before and they knew what it was like so Union J were very appreciative of anything they could say to make the experience a little easier.

'You know, you can sing the song – you've been practising all week, so just get out there,' said Niall. 'Just be yourselves the whole time.'

And shaggy-haired heartthrob Harry Styles had some

important words for baby-faced George. He told him: 'Never cut your curls.'

The pep talk had really given the boys the confidence boost they needed to go out on stage and fight for their place in the competition. They'd practised for hours, but would that be enough?

Standing on a huge plinth, with their new name emblazoned on it, the pressure was on. This was it. This was finally their moment. This was where they would prove to their mentor Louis that he had made the right decision. This was where they would prove to the other judges that they deserved to be in the competition. And this was where they would win the hearts of the eight million viewers at home.

'Tonight, I'm gonna have myself a real good time…'

George was the first to sing, to the appreciation of the audience, before he was joined one by one by Josh, JJ and Jaymi, all singing the Queen classic.

'If you wanna have a good time, just give me a call…' they sang and if any of the girls watching at home knew their numbers, they would certainly have been dialling.

After they'd sung a few lines, the stage was swarming with brightly dressed backing dancers and pyrotechnics and you could hardly see the boys against all that was going on. With so many scantily clad dancers gyrating in front of them, it was a wonder they could concentrate.

Tulisa looked stony faced as the boys belted out the tune but Union J were oblivious, lost in the excitement of the moment – their first ever, live, on-stage performance. When they finished, they jumped energetically down from their plinth and walked towards the judges, the cheers deafening them.

Tulisa began to speak, signalling for the audience to quieten down. It was time to hear what the judges had to say.

'Guys, it pains me to say this and I know the audience are going to disagree with me, but I just wasn't feeling that tonight. I don't think you're at your full potential.'

At this the mood in the arena changed and the cheers instantly turned to boos. The boys' hearts began to race – this wasn't sounding good.

'I didn't agree with that song choice, Louis – I really didn't,' Tulisa continued, focusing her attention on the boys' mentor.

'There was so much going on and what was important, which was the vocals, was missing,' she added, ignoring the angry fans behind her. Then she said the words that the boys had been dreading: 'If you get through to next week, I need to hear vocals.'

If…? It was a shocking start to the competition for the new foursome and somewhere deep down they must have started to worry that their dreams would be over as quickly as they'd begun.

'Louis, what were you thinking?' Tulisa went on, getting more and more angry at her fellow judge. 'They're young and they're fresh, and you've made them feel so dated.'

It was a damning appraisal of all their hard work and Union J looked devastated.

Louis sounded unconvinced as he tried to defend himself.

'I gave them a big task with Queen, okay, but listen – it's fun, like something out of *Glee*…'

But Tulisa couldn't bear to hear anymore.

'Boys,' she said kindly, 'all the faults as far as I'm concerned aren't yours, it's down to Louis.'

It was small comfort to Union J, who knew that it didn't matter whose fault it was: if nobody voted for them, they were done for.

Gary decided to step in, but it wasn't good news from him either.

'I have to agree, Tulisa. And guys, I want to say this – you're a good band and I thought, Louis, that putting George in was a genius move, but you have to smooth them out. That was a catastrophic song choice and an awful version. It was so dated with the dancers.'

Then he turned to the Irish judge and said harshly: 'Since you worked in the business, boy bands have changed.'

In the face of this verbal onslaught, Louis gave up defending himself and the boys and eventually had to agree with Tulisa and Gary.

'You know what,' he said quietly, 'I think the song choice wasn't great, it was too big for you.' Then he whined: 'But it's only Week One!'

Back and forth the arguments went. Tulisa was quite clearly angry with Louis and felt as their mentor, he'd let the boys down. Meanwhile, Louis tried to calm the raging fury directed at him by promising to do better the next week. But by now the boys must have been seriously wondering if there would even be a next week.

'I didn't want to play it safe,' Louis sulked. 'You're all playing it too safe.'

'I didn't play it safe,' said an indignant Tulisa, 'I had someone singing their own song!' she almost yelled.

She was referring to Lucy Spraggan, who had impressed the judges earlier in the show by singing her own composition, 'Mountains'.

It was as if the judges didn't even realise that the poor boys were standing on stage, where they must have been feeling very exposed. Surely they were praying it would end soon, so they could run away and hide!

Finally, Nicole put an end to the fighting. 'Well done boys for performing as a group for the very first time, live on television,' she said, hearing the booing instantly turn to cheers behind her. She went on to say that she agreed with Gary and Tulisa, though – which meant not one of the judges had really liked their first ever performance.

Louis tried to salvage the night for the boys as he could see that it was probably very lonely and scary up on stage, listening to such a landslide of criticism.

'Guys, you know what, let's hope everybody at home votes for you and we will do better next week. We're prepared to work hard…'

But it wasn't the most confident of pep talks, and the boys must have felt that their mentor had badly let them down.

'To be fair, we did the best we could with the song choice,' said JJ, the first of the boys to speak since their disastrous song.

Huddled together, George put his arm around his new bandmate for moral support as he continued: 'Like Louis says, maybe next time we'll try a different song. We're just praying that everyone votes for us.'

George tried to speak next, his face the picture of sorrow. But before he'd got one single word out, the previously silent audience began to scream their love for him. Blushing, he smiled for the first time since the awful judges' comments had begun and his beautiful face lit up. It was the boost he needed to continue.

'We're going to take on board what you've said to us and hopefully if we get through to next week we're going to do better,' he said in a determined voice.

But they had to get through first, and after being slated by the judges, it was going to be very difficult.

As they listened to Dermot O'Leary call out the number

to vote for Union J, the boys waved and left the stage, their heads bowed and their hearts heavy.

> **DID YOU KNOW?**
>
> Union J's Josh says his main influences are Chris Brown, Tinie Tempah, Bruno Mars… and Michael Bublé!

After everyone had sung, George, Jaymi, Josh and JJ reflected on the evening. MK1 had picked up the pace and did a cool mash-up of Chipmunk and Hot Chocolate, strutting confidently around the stage, but their vocals weren't perfect.

Jade Ellis had put her sultry tones to good use, singing the Enrique Iglesias' ballad 'Hero', while Ella Henderson, who was fast becoming one of the boys' best friends, had sung Gary Barlow's 'Rule the World' to high praise.

Gary had even said: 'I've got to be honest, there's nothing I hate more than someone singing my song ten times better than me.'

The Union J boys were facing some stiff competition.

After a sleepless night and a restless day, they were back at the studio for the live results show. Thirteen acts would be cut down to twelve and the boys were praying that they wouldn't be the first to leave.

'Backstage, the nerves are jingling and jangling,' said Dermot O'Leary, opening the show – and he was spot on.

After joining with the other contestants to sing Emeli Sandé's 'Read All About It', the audience was treated to performances from former *X Factor* winner Leona Lewis and RnB star Ne-Yo. It was a bit of light relief, but the waiting was torture.

Finally, it was time to face the music.

The two acts with the fewest votes would be singing for their survival; one of them would be going home. The boys could only hope it wouldn't be them.

All the acts stood on the stage, trying to stop themselves from shaking. Standing next to Louis, Union J looked nervous.

Dermot O'Leary started speaking.

'In no particular order, the first act going through to next week is….'

There was a tense pause.

'…Kye.'

'Also through is James,' he said next.

'And District 3…'

The Union J boys hadn't heard their names being called and the odds were getting slimmer. But then…

'The next act through to next week is Union J!'

The audience exploded into cheers and the boys began jumping up and down with uncontrollable excitement. Jumping on Louis, who looked mightily relieved, they hugged him tight.

In the end, Rylan and Carolynne found themselves in the bottom two, and they both had to sing again for the judges.

Rylan sang 'One Night Only' from the musical *Dreamgirls*, and Carolynne sang 'There You'll Be' by country star Faith Hill.

But tensions were simmering between the judges.

Gary had taken an instant dislike to Rylan the night before, telling him: 'I really was having fun till you started singing.'

Nicole had made everyone laugh by telling Gary: 'Don't be an old grumpy fart now…'

But when Louis chose not to save Carolynne, which took the vote to deadlock, Gary was enraged. He couldn't understand why Louis wouldn't save the talented songstress over fun performer Rylan.

It wasn't Carolynne's night. At the mercy of the public vote she was sent home, prompting Gary to storm off the stage, angrily telling the camera crew: 'Get the camera out of my face!'

Even Rylan was in tears over Gary's impromptu rage. 'Get me somewhere else,' he wept, walking backstage to where his stunned fellow contestants were waiting.

Union J were first to comfort him. 'I just want to walk out!' sobbed Rylan. 'No, you don't,' soothed George sympathetically. 'You deserve to be here, they saved you.'

Everyone agreed.

Later that night the mood was lifted as all the remaining acts laughed and joked with Caroline Flack and Olly Murs on *The Xtra Factor*.

Jade Ellis revealed she was terrified of spiders and Lucy Spraggan said she hated chewing gum. While James Arthur told everyone how much he hated cricket, joking: 'How hard is it to hit a ball with a stick?' – before being handed a bat and failing miserably to hit a ball at least five times, much to the audience's amusement.

But all eyes were on Ella Henderson when a fan called the show and said to her: 'You're living with a lot of really hot boys at the moment – out of all of them which one do you fancy the most?'

Ella went red and struggled to think of the right answer.

She wasn't helped when Caroline Flack and the other contestants all started mumbling and coughing 'George!' under their breath.

'I get along with all the guys, right,' she said, diplomatically, trying to avoid answering the question.

'Come on,' teased Caroline. 'If you *had* to fancy one, who would it be?'

'This is going to spiral into something, isn't it?' she said, sighing. 'Right, my best friend is George...' she admitted, to delighted whoops and some teasing laughter.

'I'll never hear the end of this now, never,' she added, prophetically.

DID YOU KNOW?

Lucy Spraggan's self-released single 'Last Night' entered the UK Singles Chart at number 11 following her *X Factor* audition.

CHAPTER SIX

LOVE BLOSSOMS

WEEK TWO ~ LOVE AND HEARTBREAK
13/14 October 2012

What Union J sang: 'Bleeding Love' – Leona Lewis/'Broken Strings' – James Morrison

What the judges said:
Tulisa: 'Guys, much better than last week.'
Nicole: 'You did everything right.'
Gary: 'What a total transformation!'
Louis: 'You can be the next big boy band in the UK if you work hard.'

Waking up on Monday morning, the boys reflected on the weekend and their first live show. It hadn't gone as well as they had hoped and it made them realise that anything could happen – they just had to be prepared for it.

They also felt they hadn't worked quite as hard as they could have done. Maybe they shouldn't have had that night out at top celeb haunt Whisky Mist. They had been acting like rock stars, but they weren't quite there yet.

This week's theme would be 'Love and Heartbreak'. It seemed so appropriate – especially since the boys were feeling pretty broken-hearted about the ear bashing they'd received the week before.

'Unfortunately, things didn't really go to plan when we got on stage,' Josh recalled. 'We genuinely, when we were up on that stage, thought we were going home.'

It was time to take stock and move on. If they let it affect this week's performance then they would be out for sure.

At the rehearsal studios, the boys sat down with their mentor Louis for a heart-to-heart. The mood was sombre.

'Boys, you're lucky to be here,' he told them. 'You've got to work twice as hard now.'

Everyone nodded in total agreement. Union J were now the underdogs of the competition and this wasn't where they wanted to be.

'We didn't put enough work into it,' George admitted. 'It's really made us realise how much we want to be in this competition and we've got a lot of work to do this week.'

Gently, Louis tried to lift their sagging spirits.

'I want you to do three things this week,' he told them. 'Rehearse, rehearse, rehearse!'

The boys got to work. First, they watched their performance and took notes on where they had gone wrong, vowing not to make the same mistakes again. They could see that it had been lifeless and old-fashioned but now they could work on turning things around.

Every single moment they practised their singing. On the stairs, in their room, in taxis – their life must have been like something out of *Glee*!

The country was clamouring for the boys' attention and they obviously had a lot to do besides rehearse. But even when they were attending interviews with magazines and newspapers, or cool photoshoots with top photographers, they used every spare second to sing together.

It was all work, work, work; the boys knew they couldn't have tried any harder. Each night they went to bed exhausted, lyrics and harmonies swimming round their heads. They also knew they had to do a lot better with their choreography, so they spent hours at the studio with choreographer Brian Friedman. It was tough going and the boys struggled.

'No, no, *no*!' Brian yelled. 'It's not good enough, we've got to do it again!'

It was Louis' battle too. After all, his reputation was at stake. He was backing the four boys and was worried he'd look past his prime if they couldn't win over the judges in their second week.

Even older fellow contestant Kye stepped in to help the boys with their song. How sweet!

'We're not going to let Louis down,' the boys agreed.

Slowly, their efforts began to pay off. After one stage rehearsal, Louis took them to one side and finally smiled.

'Guys, that was good! You're starting to look like a real pop group…'

DID YOU KNOW?

Union J's Josh says his favourite food is pizza and his favourite place to go on holiday is St Lucia – where Tulisa took her acts in the Judges' Houses stage. Unlucky!

In his rare moments without the other boys, George managed to find time to spend with 16-year-old starlet Ella Henderson. Rumours had been flying about the couple being in an *X Factor* romance and the national newspapers and magazines were filled with gossip.

And the duo didn't do much to make those rumours go away. They played thumb wars in the hotel bar, their hands locked together as they dissolved in fits of giggles. And they chatted in their jim-jams on George's bed, totally engrossed in each other.

Ella flatly denied anything was going on, though. 'Let's clear something up,' she said to the *X Factor* cameras. 'George and I, we've got so much in common with each other, we do spend a lot of time with each other, but I don't get why it has to be the *X Factor* romance, because it's really not.'

But her face was bright red and she kept laughing as she spoke, so it wasn't the most convincing speech.

She visited her mentor Tulisa on the set of the music video she was shooting and asked for some advice.

'Every single guy that I'm seen with, I'm automatically having a relationship with,' Tulisa confided to the teen. 'It drives me mad!'

'I'll just laugh it off,' Ella decided.

But it wasn't just George she was supposed to be cosying

up to – according to some newspapers, it was District 3's Dan, too!

Perhaps the boy bands' musical battle would spill over into their personal lives as well…

But if love was blossoming anywhere in the *X Factor* Hotel it would only help them with that week's songs. They would surely be emotional and heartfelt tracks and tender-aged Ella – who said she'd never been in love – was worried that she wouldn't be able to really feel the emotion needed to do her song justice. Maybe a bit of harmless flirting with the other boys would give her the inspiration she needed on stage.

Finally, the live show began, with Dermot O'Leary bouncing onto the stage to the sound of 'Firework'.

'The boys have been rehearsing all week and I'm going to show Gary Barlow that I know a lot more about boy bands than he thinks,' said Louis.

Clearly the tension between the two judges after their bust-up over Carolynne Poole hadn't disappeared completely.

So, what would the judges be like towards each other this week?

'Let's show Gary "Borelow" what he's been waiting for!' Nicole told a nervous Rylan before the show.

'When two tribes go to war…' went the opening song, as the stage doors opened and Gary, Nicole, Tulisa and Louis walked out. Gary was certainly standing a step further away than the other judges and the audience was nervous.

Time to clear the air, and peacemaker Dermot O'Leary, well accustomed to the judges' tantrums, made it happen by asking what had happened the week before.

'I just couldn't make up my mind,' admitted a distressed-looking Louis. 'Carolynne was the better singer, but Rylan's such an entertainer.'

'Gary, have you forgiven Louis?' Dermot asked.

There was a pause. 'Absolutely,' he said, standing up. 'This is a new day, let's shake hands.'

Everyone was visibly relieved. It was all about the acts, after all, not the judges. Sometimes they seemed to forget that.

Making up out of the way, it was time for the show to go on…

DID YOU KNOW?

Gary's mum told him off for rowing with fellow judge Louis Walsh. Gary told the *People* newspaper that he'd got a dressing down from Marge, who said: 'You shouldn't do that – he's older than you and you should show him some respect.' Too right!

Backstage, the boys were nervous. It was a big moment for them: they had to shine this week or it might mean the end of their *X Factor* journey.

As Louis introduced them, their backing music began. Dressed in cute winter coats and scarves, and standing against a stunning backdrop of bare winter trees, the boys sounded instantly better than the week before.

They sang Leona Lewis's 'Bleeding Love' so well that it sounded like it was their own composition. A few minutes later they moved seamlessly into 'Broken Strings', and the crowd screamed themselves hoarse. As they walked over to the audience and sang the words directly to their fans, it was clear the boys had listened to Nicole the week before when she told them to interact with the crowds more.

As the song ended, they knew in their hearts that it had been a much better performance than last week's disaster. But

Propelled into stardom. Jaymi Hensley enjoying *X Factor* fame at the film premiere of *The Twilight Saga: Breaking Dawn Part 2.*

Life has changed dramatically for the boys since entering *The X Factor*.
JJ Hamblett at the *Cosmopolitan* Ultimate Women Awards 2012.

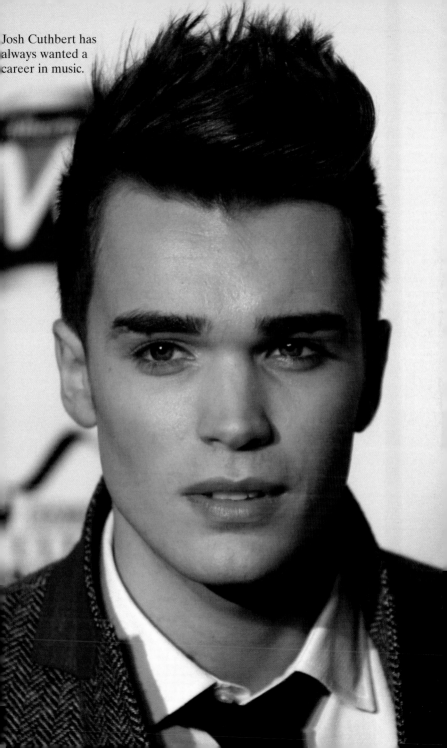

Josh Cuthbert has
always wanted a
career in music.

A second chance for George.
After auditioning as a solo artist for *The X Factor* and being axed at
Bootcamp, George Shelley was asked to join the boys in Triple J,
consequently changed to Union J.

A busy day at the studio.

Above: Fans wait outside the *X Factor* studios for their arrival.

Below left: George at St Pancras International with fellow contestant Ella Henderson.

Below right: Arriving at the studio together, ready to rehearse.

Good friends.

Above left: Celebrating Rylan Clark's birthday at Mahiki, London, with fellow contestants District 3.

Above right: Taking fame in their stride at an award ceremony.

Below: Out and about in London together.

Looking the part. Invitations to big events have become a regular occurrence for the band since being on *The X Factor*.

Above: The boys pose at the Ultimate Women Awards.

Below left: Taking time out from attending events.

Below right: On the red carpet.

Tulisa Contostavlos posing with Louis Walsh, mentor to Union J and District 3.

it wasn't their own opinion that mattered – now it was down to the judges…

Tulisa's grin was the first sign that things would be okay. 'Guys, much better than last week,' she said. 'Much better song choice and most importantly, I can hear your vocals and that's what I wanted.'

As she took a breath to continue, she found herself struggling to speak over the cheers from behind her. 'I know you guys have a really strong female following,' she added, 'so you've got a lot of potential to do well in this competition.'

George visibly breathed a huge sigh of relief and JJ, Jaymi and Josh all broke out into smiles.

Gary smiled too. 'Okay, what a transformation from last week,' he said kindly, before taking another verbal swipe at his fellow judge. 'I thought Louis really let you down with the song choice last week – am I right in thinking that Kye helped you with the song tonight?'

The boys nodded gratefully.

'Okay good,' Gary continued. 'In future don't listen to Louis, listen to Kye. Well done, boys, congratulations!'

Louis chose to rise above the snipe, and all his face revealed was the pride he was obviously feeling.

Nicole wasn't smiling as she began: 'Boys, I hate to be the one to break it to you, but…

'…you got everything right this week!'

In shock at their resounding success, the boys started punching the air with happiness. 'You stripped everything back, it was beautiful, it was simple. If you keep growing and performing like that you're going to be selling out the O2 one day.'

JJ couldn't stay silent and a loud 'Wow!' escaped his lips.

It was left to Louis to sum up the judges' feelings on Union J's second live performance.

'Guys, you worked so hard this week and it so paid off! You're like a new group, and you bring something to this show that no one else is bringing – excitement. I can feel it in the studio.'

And he was right. The air was positively crackling with it.

'Guys, you know what? You can be the next big boy band in the UK if you work hard.'

The boys were dumbstruck at all the praise they were getting. For a few moments all they could say was thank you. Then they realised they were on live television and that millions of people were waiting for them to speak.

'This week the judges' comments have put a massive smile on all of our faces,' said Josh.

As George opened his mouth to agree, the audience went bananas, screaming out his name and making him blush – just as the week before.

'These comments are going to push us even harder,' he finally managed.

Dermot started to laugh. 'I do get the impression,' he said. 'That George, you could pretty much say anything and girls would scream in this audience!'

It was a nice note to end on, and with that the boys walked off stage, buzzing with their newfound confidence. Last week, the boy band battle had been won by District 3. Would this week belong to Union J?

DID YOU KNOW?

Carolynne Poole, who was the first to leave in Season Nine after losing the sing-off to Rylan Clark, has auditioned for *X Factor* before. She reached the Judges' House stage in Season Eight.

Ella Henderson sang next and once again blew the judges away with a stunning rendition of 'Loving You' by Minnie Ripperton. It was jazzy and fresh, while being soulful and full of power.

When it was time for Rylan to sing, even the audience was nervous. Gary and Louis had made up after last week's fighting over him, but what would Gary think of him this week?

The stage darkened and as a familiar and simple piano tune started up, all the acts, including the Union J boys, wondered what Rylan would sing – and whether Gary would soften towards the former model.

'I guess now it's time for me to give up...' he began soulfully.

Gary's jaw dropped.

Rylan was singing a Take That song!

In homes all over the UK, people gasped at his bravery. But then the music stopped abruptly.

'I ain't singing it, really,' the cheeky singer said in his loveable Essex drawl. 'That was just for you, Gary', he added, grinning.

Gary couldn't help himself. Rylan had pranked him good and he chuckled away, along with the audience. Before he could say anything, Rylan's real music started and as the beat on which he thrived kicked in, he put on a show that had everyone dancing in the aisles.

It was an energetic performance of 'Groove Is In The Heart' and summer club anthem 'Gangnam Style' and the audience enjoyed watching him prance around the stage surrounded by his dancers. 'Let's have some fun, *X Factor*!' he yelled halfway through, and Nicole obliged him by getting up and dancing, too.

Rylan may not have had the best voice – a fact he himself would admit – but there was no denying he was popular. He knew just how to liven up a crowd.

Pink balloons rained down as he finished and Louis described his performance as 'entertainment with a capital "E"'.

But there was silence from Gary, who was met by a wall of boos before he even spoke – he was definitely turning into the pantomime villain of the *X Factor* season.

'Rylan, if this was a competition for how many songs you could kill in two minutes, you would win hands down,' he said.

Thick-skinned Rylan laughed it off – he had seen this coming.

'Interestingly,' Gary continued, 'when you started off, actually the best bit was my song. After that it became this musical dirge to cover up the fact that you can't sing.'

Ouch!

Time to get real. 'Look, I'm never gonna like this, okay? I hear from everyone backstage that you're a lovely guy and I'm sure if we sat and had a drink together I may well enjoy it – for about thirty seconds,' he said.

Everyone felt sorry for the poor lad but Rylan recovered quickly and quipped: 'Gary, I was a little bit worried, actually. I booked you a cab, just in case you, er, walked out!'

Everyone laughed at Gary's expense.

'That's funny,' Gary shot back. 'I've had yours on hold for two weeks now…'

Clearly there was no love lost between them. And if Gary would just admit it to himself, maybe one reason why he struggled to like Rylan was because with his stage presence, he reminded Gary an awful lot of someone he used to work with. Someone he had also spectacularly fallen out with…

But in any case, Rylan's act had cheered all the contestants up. It was the light relief that everyone, including Union J, had needed.

DID YOU KNOW?

George Shelley was born a blonde! Early pics show he had the cutest pudding-bowl haircut.

Backstage, all the acts were doing a great job of pretending they weren't a bag of nerves but District 3 were more nervous than most. After the success of the week before, they'd had an awful five days' rehearsing. They weren't very confident at all and when they took to the stage it showed.

The judges weren't impressed with their rendition of 'I Swear', by All4One. And the next night it was their turn to be in the bottom two, along with Melanie Masson.

Although they survived to go through to Week Three, this particular round of the battle of the boy bands had definitely gone to Union J.

CHAPTER SEVEN

STARDOM BECKONS

WEEK THREE ~ CLUB CLASSICS
20/21 October 2012

What Union J sang: 'When Love Takes Over' – David Guetta

What the judges said:
Tulisa: 'I knew I saw that potential in you.'
Gary: 'I think we are witnessing the birth of a new boy band.'
Nicole: 'You're very cool and effortless.'
Louis: 'This band has got a massive future.'

This week, loyal Union J fans were dealt a huge blow when they found out that the only member of the band who was still single was lovely George.

'I'm sort of early stage seeing someone,' Josh told *Star*

Magazine. JJ said he was in the same situation. Jaymi spoke about his long-term relationship, before George happily announced: 'I'm single,' completely ignoring the rumours about himself and Ella Henderson.

George also said he was loving the attention all the boys were getting. 'It's great,' he admitted. 'It's crazy to think how we've gone from being normal to having fans following us everywhere.'

And JJ – who George, Josh and Jaymi once pushed onto their hotel balcony naked, to the delight of their fans – agreed. 'We had fans waiting outside our hotel for nine hours the other day. They're constantly tweeting us, saying: "When are you coming down again?"'

As often as they could, the boys made sure they'd go down and say hi – and even helped take pictures of themselves for the hundreds of patient JCats. They had to, really, because huge steeled gates and fences had been put up to keep the acts separate from the thousands of fans.

Everywhere they went, the boys were asked for photographs and autographs – even while they were once out shopping in Topshop. A posse of excited girls followed them around the store before throwing their arms around the boys for hugs.

George tried on some silly glasses and posed, asking: 'What do you think?'

But even in funny specs he still looked gorgeous.

Teddy bears and love notes were being delivered to their hotel daily, and while the boys thought it was great, Louis was becoming increasingly concerned that all the female attention would distract the boys. As their mentor, he sat them down for a heartfelt chat.

'Who gets the most girls?' he asked them one morning

in the rehearsal studio. He understood that it wasn't their fault that they were so adored – they couldn't help being handsome and talented.

'Josh and George,' replied JJ, immediately.

'I know there's hundreds of girls screaming for you outside but don't get distracted,' Louis told them, wisely.

'You've got a long way to go yet and an awful lot of hard work.'

'It was really hard last week,' said Jaymi, in a serious voice. 'We can't rest on that, because if we slip slightly people might not believe in us. We've got to work ten times harder.'

George looked sincere as he added: 'With the support we've been getting, it's really important for us to go out there and not let anyone down.'

Everyone agreed. Louis had said his piece and the boys appreciated it. They all high-fived and went off to rehearse.

But not everyone was taking the competition so seriously. Rylan Clark and Lucy Spraggan found themselves in big trouble after they went out following Sunday's results show and got staggeringly drunk.

They were so excited to discover that they were still in the competition that they'd gone to the famous London club G.A.Y and drank far too much. When they got back to the hotel, they made such a racket that the show's bosses were not at all impressed. Especially since the paparazzi had been waiting for them and had caught the whole thing on camera.

They were screaming and shouting, swearing and smoking – which is bad for your voice, let alone your health – and the pair had totally embarrassed themselves. Rylan nearly got naked and Lucy was videoed picking him up and carrying him around. They were obviously so drunk they had no idea what they were doing. It was an awful example to set the younger contestants – and their fans.

The pair of them got an almighty telling-off, and as punishment they were moved from the swanky Corinthia Hotel to a Hilton in Wembley – to get them away from the other acts. Oops!

They were now very far from the glitzy London nightlife they'd been enjoying. Instead they were much closer to the studio, so that their mentors could keep a closer eye on them.

Lucy was upset and tweeted that she'd had a miserable week. The *Mirror* reported that Tulisa had read her the riot act, accusing poor Lucy of not taking the competition seriously enough and throwing away a great opportunity.

But Rylan didn't seem bothered at all and tweeted: 'We've been naughty so we're going to the Attitude mag after party!!!'

The cheeky Essex boy wasn't taking any notice of the judges and was determined to have a good time.

DID YOU KNOW?

Union J's Josh loves Nando's. He always orders a half peri-peri chicken and chips. Yum!

After a lot of practising, the boys found themselves at the *X Factor* studios for yet another live show. It was amazing to them that they'd got this far – but it wasn't so amazing for everyone watching the show at home. They were naturals!

They began their performance by sitting quietly on stage, before Josh started singing: 'When Love Takes Over'. Then, with a quick key change, lights started flashing, the beat kicked in and all four boys got up and danced their socks off.

Tulisa absolutely loved it. 'Guys, I'm so happy! I knew I saw this potential in you – you are finally finding your feet in the competition,' she said.

'Each week you're getting better and better and better. And your female fanbase is getting stronger and stronger and stronger.'

The boys were so pleased they had to stop themselves from jumping up and down right there on the stage. But Tulisa wasn't finished. 'This is just the beginning for you guys. That was a wicked performance tonight – I can just see it getting better each week,' she concluded, leaving the boys buzzing with confidence.

Gary took a pause before he gave his verdict. 'I think we are witnessing the birth of a brand new boy band right here,' he said, looking very pleased with the lads. But then he added: 'Just a little bit of technical stuff – you sound great when you sing individually, I could just do with a little more harmony.'

But the boys could see that this was constructive criticism and were happy to take the seasoned singer's advice.

Nicole had some reservations, too. 'The reason why I like you guys and why we all like you so much is you're very cool and effortless when you perform,' she began, adding to everyone else's praise. 'But this is Club Classics... I need more energy, boys – you were still singing the song like you were singing the ballad last week. I need more energy and we need a harmony. We had four people singing in unison.'

More valuable advice. District 3 had their harmonies down to a fine art form. It would be tough to challenge them, but Union J would certainly try.

Louis gave his usual proud father face and said: 'Guys, it's working! The hard work is paying off. There's a great chemistry, there's great fun and the image – guys, it's coming together.'

It was only Week Three and the boys were doing so well, especially since they'd not been a band for very long at all. In such a short space of time, they were capturing the public's hearts – no easy feat.

The boys were pleased, but humble. Dermot O'Leary asked them what they thought and Josh said: 'Yeah, really happy, obviously we've got a lot to work on still, but we're new and we're hoping to develop.'

And with that they left the stage.

Next, Lucy Spraggan and Rylan Clark took to the stage one after another with their usual gusto. As usual, Rylan caused arguments between all the judges with his performance of club classics 'On The Floor', 'Don't Stop The Music' and 'I See You Baby'.

Earlier in the week, his mentor Nicole had given an exclusive interview to the *Mirror*, where she spoke about how she would defend Rylan until the bitter end and protect him from his harshest critic: Gary Barlow. She also spoke about the pressures of the show, which the contestants were doing a great job of hiding – or at least they had been, until last week.

Poor James Arthur had suffered a panic attack and thought he was seriously ill. An ambulance was called and he was treated at the scene, but it gave all the acts something to think about.

The Union J boys had each other to rely on and confide in, which must have helped, but the pressure was still very intense. Nicole told the *Mirror*: 'People watch it on TV but they don't realise what goes on behind the scenes and how much pressure they were under.'

She went on: 'This is what happens when you are thrown into an environment you're not used to. You are working every single day, non-stop. He is around new people...

Getting your glasses taken away from you, spray-tanned, hair cut – it is a completely different world.'

James's experience was scary for everyone and a warning to work hard, but not overdo it.

On the results show 24 hours later, the acts all sang Chaka Khan's 'Ain't Nobody' together and the stage vibrated with energy. Superstars Emeli Sandé and Labrinth performed next, before former *X Factor* contestants JLS sang their new single, 'Hottest Girl In The World'. It was inspirational for all the acts, but especially Union J and District 3. Both were aspiring to be just as successful as the top band, if not more.

Then Dermot O'Leary took to the stage and said: 'Okay, it's time for the results.'

Would their hard work pay off? Were they going through to the next live show? They couldn't wait to find out...

Dermot soon put them out of their misery.

'The first act returning is Union J!'

The boys screamed and jumped up and down, hugging each other tight. Then they threw their arms around Louis and the other groups before Dermot had the chance to continue announcing which of the acts was safe for another week.

One by one, everyone celebrated their survival – apart from MK1 and Kye Sones, who found themselves in the bottom two. And after a tense sing-off, it was time for MK1 to go home.

DID YOU KNOW?

MK1's Sim turned down a football scholarship in America to study Music Industry Management at Buckinghamshire University. Now that's dedication!

CHAPTER EIGHT

THE FAN
MADNESS BEGINS

WEEK FOUR ~ HALLOWEEN
27/28 October 2012

What Union J sang: 'Sweet Dreams' – Beyoncé/'Perfect' –
Pink

What the judges said:
Tulisa: 'Jaymi, you have a seriously powerful voice.'
Nicole: 'I thought that was absolute perfection.'
Gary: 'I've kind of seen this performance before.'
Louis: 'I know you can perform more.'

Safe in their cosy hotel room, the boys looked out of the
window and saw a familiar sight: girls camped outside in
the freezing cold, hoping to catch a glimpse of their new

heroes. They'd been there for weeks now, starting out as a small group, which had slowly grown as the weeks had passed. Some of them had even managed to break in, sneaking past the huge bodyguards on the doors and surprising the boys outside their bedrooms – while wearing their favourite onesies!

As much as the boys appreciated their fans, it was quite a shock to see them in the privacy of their hotel. Some of the girls had even been really clever and sent their CVs to the hotel, hoping to get jobs in the bar.

The boys felt a little bit like they were being chased. They could no longer leave the hotel through the front doors because they were always mobbed, so they had started to leave by the secret back exit.

Some girls were even sleeping outside the hotel. It was crazy and the boys were worried about them. 'Where are their mums?' they asked each other, shocked.

'We could see them trying to work out which room we were in,' Josh told the *Sun* newspaper. 'They were removed by two beefy security lads.'

George added: 'We're just normal guys doing our thing and it's crazy to think girls would chase us around and want to be near us all the time.'

They were quick to point out that they all thought it was lovely that everyone was supporting them, but show bosses were still concerned. They decided to draft in extra security for the lads, just in case.

The boys took some time out from rehearsals to attend Rylan's Halloween themed birthday party, dressing as scary surgeons. Poor Ella couldn't go because she was too young, so the boys went on a spooky bus tour of London too, so she wouldn't feel left out.

Ella was sitting next to Josh, and everyone was screaming as the bus tour guides told them spooky stories and kept making them jump. The boys all screamed like big girls!

George decided to speak to *Now* magazine about his newfound fame, and said that he was struggling with being described as such a ladies' man.

'I know the others would say I'm the womaniser of the group but I wouldn't describe myself as that,' the magazine reported.

George has often been compared to One Direction's Harry Styles. But in the interview he said that despite having the same floppy hair, beautiful lips and face of an angel, he was a bit upset when he came face to face with Harry and discovered that actually they look nothing alike!

'We were doing a photoshoot and I bumped into Harry Styles,' he said. 'I have to say I was gutted, as despite being compared to him, I look nothing like him!'

There's room in our lives for both of you, George.

Previously, the judges had told JJ, Jaymi, Josh and George that they wanted to hear more harmonies and see more energy. Union J knew that the District 3 boys had great harmonies and they needed to work on their own, so they practised and practised.

And they were exhausted after going over and over their dance steps. When the big night came, they were going to be ready…

DID YOU KNOW?

Ella Henderson took her GCSEs at almost the same time as singing at her *X Factor* audition but she still managed to get seven, including an A in music.

Sitting on a car in dark outfits, the boys looked sultry as they began to sing Beyoncé's 'Sweet Dreams' to the judges. Their voices were beautiful and when they leapt effortlessly down from the vehicle they looked really cool. Then suddenly they were leaping all over the place, confidently singing to a few very lucky girls in the audience, and storming the stage as if it was a massive stadium gig! But when they finished and the cheers died down, they were in for a shock.

Tulisa began.

'Guys, I think the vocals were really good tonight. Jaymi, you were particularly strong – you have a seriously powerful voice,' she said, praising the cutie. 'My only issue tonight was that in the past two weeks you've improved so much that I'm kind of waiting for you to get better. And I felt like you played it just a little bit safe tonight.'

Gary agreed. He called it 'overproduced' and said he could tell everyone loved the performance, but he thought it was 'safe'.

'Come back with something different next week and change it up,' he advised.

Nicole loved it, though, calling it absolute perfection. 'I love every single one of you,' she gushed. 'You stand there, you own it, you pay attention to the girls, you're honest... It was simple, it was beautiful – I don't know what all the fuss is about.'

But although the American judge-performer had loved their song, Louis gave the boys a shock when he said: 'Guys, it was great but I know you can perform more. I believe in this group so much, I don't want them in the bottom two.'

He looked worried as he appealed to everyone to vote for the act. It was a mixed group of comments and the boys didn't know what to think. They had no idea whether or not they were safe and had a sneaking suspicion that there would be tough times ahead.

'We took your comments on board about the harmonies,' said Josh. 'So we really tried to work on that and we sort of gave it our best.'

His fellow singers nodded in agreement when he added: 'And we're hopefully gonna develop week in, week out.'

One act was missing from the line-up in Week Four – Lucy Spraggan had fallen ill and couldn't sing. She was automatically put through to the next round, making lots of Union J and District 3 fans angry. They thought it was quite unfair, but it wasn't Lucy's fault.

Rylan had enjoyed the week of his life – not only did he have a birthday party, but Robbie Williams had lavished him with attention. Gary Barlow's bandmate spent lots of time helping Rylan with his act and even had a special message for Gary.

'Gaz, I don't know what this man has done to offend you so much. I am a big, big fan,' Robbie told the cameras. 'And I don't understand how you are missing the obvious brilliance and talent of Rylan, but I'm not. I'm team Rylan all the way,' he added, as Rylan looked chuffed behind him.

Rylan sang Britney Spears' 'Toxic', and it was brilliant.

Gary might have been a little offended by it all, though because he was quite mean to Tulisa that night.

She had blamed Gary for Christopher Maloney's dodgy song choices and after a brooding silence, Gary told her: 'Tulisa, I don't know what's offended me more tonight – what you've said or your fag-ash breath.'

He even wafted his hand in front of his face for effect.

Tulisa was shocked and stared with her mouth open at the camera. She stewed while Gary spoke to his act, but it wasn't long before she hit back at him, saying: 'Lay off the red wine, Gary, because I can really smell that as well.'

Miaow! At least all the acts were getting on, because the judges were acting like children.

The next night, Robbie Williams entertained all the acts at the live results show, singing his new song, 'Candy'. But the mood dropped when it was time to find out who would be singing for survival.

It was a disaster for the boys.

Everyone was safe apart from Jade Ellis – and Union J. The poor lads were in the bottom two...

Obviously nervous, they took to the stage to sing 'Perfect' by Pink. They sang their hearts out but then so did Jade, with a beautiful rendition of Dido's 'White Flag'.

No one had a clue who was going to leave and the boys looked terrified as they stood on stage with Dermot O'Leary and Jade, waiting for the verdict.

Louis went first and obviously sent Jade home, saying: 'I'm the mentor for Union J – I love them. I don't want to lose them.'

Tulisa was next and looked very sad. It was as if she knew what was coming.

'This is easy for me,' she said. 'That's my girl up there, she sang her heart out tonight. The act I'm sending home is Union J.'

It was one vote each – what would the other judges have to say?

'Jade, you are a beautiful, beautiful young woman – a strong young woman, who has been through so much,' said Nicole. 'I know that whatever happens you're gonna get a recording deal because you're a recording artist and a brilliant one.'

Jaymi's bottom lip started to quiver and George looked

crushed as Nicole praised the talented female singer. Were they going home?

'Union J, you boys, through your performance and through your work have proven yourself to me, so the act I'm sending home, I'm sorry, is Jade.'

Relief flooded their faces – now it was all down to Gary, who hadn't always been their biggest fan.

'Guys, I have been tough on you,' he started. 'You know I'm a band member myself and every week you've come on this show, you know it's been good but it's not been exceptional…'

Jaymi, Josh, JJ and George tried to stay strong but they must have been feeling sick with worry at this point. They were loving being on the show and didn't want it to end.

'Jade, you are a phenomenal vocalist, you really are and you really sang your heart out. But I just wonder whether I want this for you more than you want it…'

Everyone was silent as he continued: 'The act I'm sending home is Jade.'

It was a mixture of happiness and sadness – Union J were through to the next week, but they would have to say goodbye to lovely Jade, something they really didn't want to do.

By now the acts were all so close there were always tears on Sunday evenings.

Tom Parker, from The Wanted, tweeted: 'Jade Ellis, you did yourself proud!'

After an emotional goodbye it was time for *The Xtra Factor* and Josh had cheered up enough to tell Caroline Flack his worst fear: wasps!

Jedward were guests on the show and they got up to their usual cheeky antics, while Ella got a surprise when Caroline and Olly Murs managed to get her beloved dog, Trixie, on Skype! The cute little doggie barked with joy when he saw Ella, who was missing him so much. But it showed that being apart from your family was one of the prices you had to pay for being in *The X Factor*.

DID YOU KNOW?

Ella's fave shop is River Island, but she also scours vintage stores for exciting one-off finds.

CHAPTER NINE

RISING FROM THE ASHES

WEEK FIVE ~ NUMBER ONES
3/4 November 2012

What Union J sang: 'Love Story' – Taylor Swift

What the judges said:
Tulisa: 'Well done, you nailed it!'
Gary: 'I thought that was a brilliant performance.'
Nicole: 'They've knocked it out of the park every week!'
Louis: 'You definitely made the right decision, saving the boys last week.'

After their bottom two showdown, the boys were feeling a bit low when they woke up the next day. But they couldn't let it affect them and as usual, Louis was on hand to talk things through.

It had all got a bit overwhelming for JJ, Josh, George and Jaymi. Their fans and the audience watching them on TV at home may have seen them as polished and professional singers, well on the road to success, but the boys just felt like normal lads with very normal backgrounds – this had been a whirlwind experience for them all.

Bright and early on Monday morning, the boys sat down with Louis in the rehearsal studios.

'I couldn't believe you were in the bottom two last week and I saw your faces,' he said, worried for his boys.

'It was a numb feeling, we didn't really know what to expect,' admitted George. 'We had to really fight to come back and sing,' said Jaymi, recalling the initial terror they'd felt before the sing-off. 'Your mouth goes dry, you're shaking, you want to be sick. You've got to use every little bit of you to come back and give a performance. Waiting to hear if you're through or not, your heart is just pounding.'

It was a very revealing conversation, and the words came straight from their hearts.

'So we've got to turn all the negativity into positive attitude,' continued Josh. 'You know – prove to the judges why we deserve to be in the competition.'

In rehearsals, Jaymi took the boys to one side and spoke to them. 'You need to take it seriously,' he told George, JJ and Josh. 'Do you want to end up where we were last week?'

They all agreed that was the last thing they wanted. This week the boys would be singing a love song and Jaymi was adamant they would make it a success.

'We just want to go out there and just have fun with it,' he told the cameras. 'Think about the first time we were in love and just go out there and let loose!'

At practise, George was seen strumming on his guitar, so

everyone knew they'd be in for a treat when the boys performed. He is a great guitarist!

Louis was nervous about the next live show, too. He told the cameras: 'I want the people at home to see the real Union J this week – we've got four very different people in the group. I don't want to see them in the bottom two again.'

They certainly are very different people, and it's lovely how well they all get on. Josh is the funny guy – all the boys think he's hilarious. Jaymi is definitely the father figure of the group; he always gives them little pep talks and is the most organised. George is the cheeky one, with his gorgeous smile, and JJ is the one who gets teased the most.

One morning Josh and George decided to make the other acts laugh by wearing their beloved onesies around the hotel and saying: 'It's "number onesies" week!' But James Arthur threw a pillow at them when they tried to record a video for *The Xtra Factor* in their favourite nightwear.

The boys love their all-in-one outfits and George never wears any boxers underneath his.

Meanwhile, Kye had been teasing Josh mercilessly about his hair – all the acts had noticed that he was constantly rearranging it, and the one thing he asked them the most was: 'Is my hair alright?'

We love your hair, Josh!

DID YOU KNOW?

The first gig that George ever attended was to see Bon Jovi, Josh's was Chris Brown, and JJ has never been to a proper gig!

Halfway through the week the boys took some time out to go to the *Mirror*'s Pride of Britain Awards, where ordinary people receive recognition for the amazing things they do. It's always an emotional event and for the boys, who are all ordinary boys really, it was particularly overwhelming.

And with emotions running high, onlookers watched as George and Ella cosied up together, fuelling the rumours about their blossoming love.

The *Mirror* reported that they were holding hands during the tear-jerking speeches, with their chairs moved away from the rest of their group's table, which included Jahmene, Kye Sones and James Arthur. And George was even seen gently stroking Ella's back and whispering to her.

They wouldn't be the first couple to get it on at The Pride of Britain Awards. Footballer Frank Lampard met Christine Bleakley there, Russell Brand and Geri Halliwell dated for a week after attending one year, and although much less successfully, former Beatle Paul McCartney met his second wife Heather Mills at the event.

Cupid obviously attends the Awards...

A source told the *Mirror*: 'They really connected when they first met, but they wanted to get to know each other before taking it up a notch. Now, after spending such an emotional evening together, they are taking things more seriously.'

Lucy Spraggan was supposed to be at rehearsals, after being off the week before, suffering from what *X Factor* officials were calling a 'severe bout of flu'. But the boys were shocked to see she wasn't there. It was looking as if she wouldn't make the live show this week, either – what would the producers do?

And there was more disaster when two days before the show, Josh woke up feeling dreadful.

The boys had eaten a Chinese takeaway the night before and Josh had scoffed his favourite prawn toast but now he was suffering with food poisoning.

While the other boys left the hotel to go and rehearse, Josh stayed in bed, tweeting: 'Haven't left my bed for the last 36 hours with food poisoning. Been so ill.'

Later, he added: 'Still feeling awful. Worrying about tomorrow.'

All their fans tweeted him their love and George, Jaymi and JJ all looked after him. But they were obviously worried that he wouldn't be okay for the live show. It would be a disaster if he couldn't perform and after being in the bottom two last week this could easily mean the end of their *X Factor* dreams.

'We're just praying that he recovers in time for the show,' tweeted JJ.

By this time, both District 3 and Union J had suffered through a sing-off and apparently tensions were rising between the two groups. Both bands knew that this week they both had to wow the judges, and as much as they liked each other as people, the national newspapers were reporting that the bands weren't really talking to each other all that much.

DID YOU KNOW?

Kye Sones is best mates with radio DJ Fearne Cotton. They met at an under-18s disco in Ruislip when they were both eleven and have been besties ever since.

Finally, it was time for the live show, and the boys appeared on stage to sing. George stepped out first, holding his guitar, followed by Josh, JJ and Jaymi, all wearing jeans and suit jackets. They looked so good in their outfits – bet there was some serious swooning in the audience that night!

Singing Taylor Swift's 'Love Story', they were pitch-perfect and as usual, the audience loved them, nearly drowning out their powerful vocals with their cheers.

It was a definite improvement on last week and the boys knew it.

'First of all,' said Tulisa, when the boys had finished, 'I would like to congratulate Louis on making such a brilliant song choice.'

Louis looked so happy. 'Well, we picked the song together,' he said proudly. 'How much have they improved?'

On stage, the boys grinned.

'Do you know what?' Tulisa continued. 'It all goes to show song choice is key, and the one thing Louis knows about is boy bands and he's trying to find your market and nail it. At the end of the day, your fans are loads of young screaming girls across the country and all they want is to see you up there, singing beautiful love songs, beautifully to them. You did that tonight. Well done, you nailed it.'

Gary was next to speak and the boys waited patiently to see what the usually strict judge had to say.

'Guys, I was concerned on Sunday that we might have made the wrong decision voting Jade off,' he began, 'but seeing how you've reacted tonight I don't think we have – I thought that was a brilliant performance.'

But he did have some criticism – about George, of all people!

'George, you fit wonderfully in the band but I think you could work on your blend just a little bit more.'

George nodded, respectfully. He wasn't going to have a tantrum when someone as knowledgeable as Gary Barlow gave him some advice.

Nicole was as pleased as everyone else to see that the boys had taken advantage of one of George's great talents. 'It's so nice to see you finally reunited with your guitar,' she told him. 'Boys, I thought that was a really solid performance. I've loved it every week. Like Tulisa said, they're singing to their fan base – good work, boys!'

On cue, the girls in the audience began screaming and the boys chuckled on stage. It was obvious that their fans really made a difference to their confidence.

'Guys, you definitely made the right decision saving the boys last week,' Louis told his fellow judges. 'Boys, you came back fighting – you've got a whole new energy.'

Dermot O'Leary asked Gary what he meant by his comment to George, and Gary joked that he had far too much hair.

Leave his curls alone, Gary!

But he explained that he meant that he wanted them to work on blending their vocals. As the boys left the stage they were chuffed to bits.

But despite their happiness, the boys were sad about one thing that night – Lucy Spraggan had decided not to return to *The X Factor*.

'I'm gutted not to be able to continue on this journey,' she said in a statement that very morning. 'To accept another free pass, having missed last weekend would not be fair on the others in the competition. I wish them all well.'

Close friend Rylan tweeted her: 'Gonna miss u being with me so much @lspraggan I love you x'.

She had been his partner-in-crime since the very beginning and he would now have to struggle on with-out her.

The mood was sombre but lightened when footage showed Nicole visiting *TOWIE* star Amy Childs' Essex salon with Rylan, so that he could get an eyebrow wax.

Nicole had never been to Essex before but learned some of the local lingo, and even practised it that night when she told Gary to 'Shuup', and that he was just 'wel jel' of Rylan.

Union J had mixed feelings when they saw District 3's performance. It wasn't their best and the judges were harsh. Would this be the week they won the battle of the boy bands? Were District 3 going home?

They'd have to wait until the next day to find out…

That night, on *The Xtra Factor*, Caroline Flack congratulated the boys on their amazing performance and asked what it was like being in the bottom two throughout the week.

'We were quite down and stuff,' said Jaymi. 'We really wanted to pick ourselves up. We went home to see our families, which really gave us a big boost. Hopefully we won't be in the bottom two tomorrow.'

Christopher Maloney revealed that JJ always eats with his mouth open and Caroline Flack asked Ella who she fancied more: Olly Murs or George Shelley?

'I don't fancy George!' she protested at the teasing.

'You don't fancy George? Yeah right!' said Caroline.

DID YOU KNOW?

The first single that JJ ever bought was Backstreet Boys' 'I Want It That Way', and Jaymi's was 'Genie In A Bottle' by Christina Aguilera.

The next night the boys were relieved to find out they were first to be declared safe from the dreaded bottom two. And surprisingly, District 3 were saved too! Obviously everyone had realised that they were fab, really – it had just been a bad night.

But Rylan and Kye Sones had to battle it out, and the judges just couldn't decide who to send home. Gary and Nicole voted to keep their own acts, and Louis voted to keep Kye, so it was down to Tulisa. 'I've got to go with my heart,' she said and opted to save Rylan. This caused a deadlock, which meant it would come down to the public vote.

Dermot opened the envelope that revealed who would be going home.

It was Kye Sones. The public were loving Rylan's entertaining performances and talented as Kye was, he just didn't have enough votes.

Gary was fuming as he took to the stage. 'Good singers go home every week,' he declared.

But it's not always so black and white on *The X Factor*. And there would be a good deal more shocks in store for everyone before the competition was over.

CHAPTER TEN

THE BATTLE OF
THE BOY BANDS

WEEK SIX ~ BEST OF BRITISH
10/11 November 2012

What Union J sang: 'Fix You' – Coldplay/'Run' – Snow Patrol

What the judges said:
Tulisa: 'Let the battle of the boy bands commence…'
Gary: 'I think something big is about to happen.'
Louis: 'Your families are so proud of you.'
Nicole: 'Beautiful song, boys – you did it justice.'

This week's performance was particularly important for Josh, JJ, Jaymi and George. Sunday would be Remembrance Day, the day when Britain takes time to honour those who have given their lives in war and conflict. All four of the boys had some kind of connection to the Armed Forces, so they really wanted to make this performance their best.

Jaymi comes from a long line of men who have served in the Royal Air Force – every male in his family has served in the RAF, going back to World War II!

Josh's dad was in the Navy for fifteen years and he's always been exceptionally proud of him for it. Josh told the *X Factor* cameras: 'It would be nice to go on stage and do something that would hopefully make him proud.'

For George the connection was even closer to home. His big brother is a Royal Marine Commando, who has completed three tours in Afghanistan.

George was just thirteen when Will first went to Afghanistan. He has said: 'It's really hard, knowing that your big brother is going out to fight for your country and he just might not come back.'

So when the boys sat down with Louis to discuss what song to sing, George told his mentor: 'It's Best of British Week – we want to dedicate our song to what we feel the best of British is, and that's the Armed Forces.'

Louis agreed, and everyone decided they would do a stripped-down version of Coldplay's 'Fix You'.

'To be honest, you need to just stand there and sing and enjoy yourselves,' said Louis. 'It works, it *really* works.'

He also wanted to praise the boys for last week's performance, which had blown all the judges away.

'You were amazing on Saturday night, that was the best performance so far,' he told them. 'I saw something brilliant, I saw a glimpse of what you could be.'

The boys were so amazed they'd made it so far in the competition. It had been so exciting and as young boys, dreaming of singing on stage, they never thought they would ever be on the *X Factor* stage with hundreds of girls screaming their names.

'We literally keep pinching ourselves,' said JJ. 'To be in this position, we couldn't ask for more.'

They began rehearsing and were determined to get the song perfect.

'George, I don't want to start off with you,' said Louis. 'I want to start off with Jaymi.' He added: 'And guys, the harmony is too loud but we're going to get it right.'

Everyone nodded. It was time for some serious hard work.

The boys were up early every day and went to bed really late. They were so tired, but hope was keeping them going. George tweeted that he had never been so tired in his entire life, while instead of going out partying, Josh snuggled up with his hot-water bottle.

They also had to do a very important photoshoot – for the winning *X Factor* single CD cover!

All of the acts had to have their pics taken, just in case they won, and Josh tweeted: 'Hopefully the next time we see the pictures it will be on that CD cover...'

And it was announced that Union J would definitely be on *The X Factor* 2012 tour, along with Ella Henderson, District 3, Christopher Maloney, Jahmene Douglas, Rylan Clark and James Arthur. It was so good to know that whoever won, everyone would be together again for a super-exciting stadium tour, just a few months away. Things were getting very real: the four boys were actually making it in the music world.

On Saturday, the boys made their way to the studio and that was when the nerves really started to kick in. Josh tweeted: 'Dress rehearsal is minutes away!! This is when I'm always dying for a wee haha!!'

And finally, it was time for them to perform.

Louis told them: 'Guys, don't forget who you're singing this to – you're singing this to your families. You're going to be great tonight.'

George replied: 'We've just got to go out there tonight and smash our performance and sing our hearts out.'

District 3 had already sung their song and received some amazing comments from the judges. How would Union J compare?

A curtain fell to reveal the boys on stage, all in black jackets and dark jeans. George strummed on his guitar while Jaymi started singing. It was very moving and their vocals were totally perfect. Their families must have been very proud – they certainly did them justice. And when it was over there must have surely been quite a few people weeping over their tea and biscuits at home.

'Louis,' began Tulisa, 'I have to confess you're on a roll tonight – you've nailed it again. Brilliant song choice, brilliant performance, what you've done tonight is you've found your market and you're very much appealing to them, so great job tonight.'

But she did have some concerns, which she went on to voice next.

'My only worry is, being honest, it's now battle of the boy bands and both bands did amazingly,' she said. 'I can't call it. My only worry is – is it going to split the votes? I don't know. Let the battle of the boy bands commence!'

The boys looked really pleased, but Tulisa was right and they knew it. There was a showdown coming, and neither band was looking forward to it.

'Good job tonight,' said Gary, 'one of my favourite songs. I thought that you all sang it really well. There's often just a little bit of pitching problems when you're blending together, just work a little bit more on that because it's all about rehearsal.'

It was advice they'd been given before and they were all trying their hardest to improve technically but unless you're an *X Factor* judge you never would have picked up on anything being wrong – the boys had sounded amazing and Gary knew it, despite his small criticisms.

'I think something big is about to happen,' he told them. 'I feel really good about you guys.'

George looked very emotional when Nicole spoke next.

'Beautiful song, boys – you did it justice. I just want to say thank you for recognising and honouring the men and women, the heroes of our Armed Forces.'

She told Jaymi his voice had shone that evening, describing it as delicate and controlled, with so much soul. It was such great praise!

'Guys, it's such a pleasure to work with four guys who work so hard. You're young, you're relevant, your families are so proud of you,' Louis told them. 'Jaymi, I know what this means for you, you've waited your whole life for this – this is your moment.'

The boys were philosophical when Dermot O'Leary asked them about their competition with District 3.

'Obviously, we're the two boy bands in the competition so obviously people are going to say there is rivalry,' said Josh. 'But everyone is in competition with each other, there's no more competition with us two than there is anyone else, so we love them to bits.'

It was very nicely said and the District 3 boys must have been glad to hear it. It's not great, being in competition with your friends.

George gave Dermot a hug and the boys left the stage.

That night, the boys went on Twitter and found that the judges weren't the only ones who loved their version of the Coldplay classic.

TOWIE's Lauren Goodger tweeted: 'I really like Union J's voices!!xx', while Katie Price wrote: 'union j are awesome defo top 3', which the boys retweeted proudly.

After the performance, the boys spent some time with their families and later that night Josh tweeted: 'I'm finally back home after a wicked night with the family :)'.

It can get lonely, staying in a hotel, even if you are with your best friends in the world. Sometimes only your family can make you feel better and having them there had made it a great night for the boys.

When they woke up the next morning, there was more than just *The X Factor* on their minds. They held a two-minute silence along with the rest of the country and tweeted: 'Love and thoughts go out to everyone who lost their lives to make the world a better place. Thank you. #RemembranceSunday'. But after that, they started to get nervous again – one more act would be leaving that evening and Union J were wishing and hoping that it wouldn't be them.

They'd received some great comments the night before, but as always, you just never knew what was going to happen.

The boys spent their time playing their favourite Pokemon game. They love it, especially Josh, who wouldn't put his Nintendo DS down! But eventually it was time to head back to the studio for the results show. And this would be the night when the Battle of the Bands would be well and truly over.

The acts were treated to Ed Sheeran singing 'Give Me Love' and Little Mix performing their new single, 'DNA'.

It was great to see how far another former *X Factor* group had come, and as the girls stormed the stage, the boys could only hope that they themselves would be there in a year's time. The night flew by and finally it was time for Dermot O'Leary to reveal the results.

It was so tense and everyone's faces showed it.

'In no particular order,' began Dermot. 'The first act through is James, then Rylan...'

Union J looked very nervous.

'...then Jahmene, then Ella...'

It was down to three acts: District 3, Union J and Christopher Maloney.

'Only one is certain of a place,' said Dermot. 'The final act returning next week is... Christopher!'

George looked close to tears and Josh, JJ and Jaymi all seemed utterly crushed.

It had come down to the moment they had all been dreading. They would have to go head to head with their friends and rivals, District 3. Only one band would survive and go through to the next live show.

The boys waited while Greg, Dan and Mickey went first. They could hear the boys singing and could also hear how nervous they were. They took the time to compose themselves, taking deep breaths and going over the lyrics in their heads. Then it was their turn to sing.

Louis introduced them, trying his hardest not to look sad. He knew what was coming – he'd have to make a decision that he'd hoped he would never have to make. 'Okay, guys, this is it, sing your hearts out – get ready for Union J!'

The boys began singing Adele's 'Set Fire To The Rain' and it was a confident performance. Despite this, Jaymi's face clearly showed the inner turmoil he was feeling. He couldn't stop now, this had been his dream his whole life. With every note he sang, he would fight.

And when it was over the boys hugged each other. Their work was done. All they could do now was listen to what the judges had to say.

Louis refused to vote – they were both his acts and he didn't want to send either of his beloved bands home. So Gary went first and when he turned to District 3, all the boys listened intently.

First, he told them that he'd thought it was going to be a simple decision, because he believed District 3 had always been better vocally. But then he told the poor lads that it had been the worst performance Greg, Dan and Mickey had done so far, and at that moment, the Union J boys knew they were in with a chance.

'Guys,' he said, turning to JJ, Josh, George and Jaymi. 'Although there were less harmonies in your performance I felt like you wanted it so much more.'

The boys were relieved when he revealed that he was sending District 3 home, but they were sad, too. They didn't like to see their friends suffering.

Nicole told District 3 that they should be proud of themselves and praised their harmonies, but then she said: 'The group that I think is a more mature group and a little bit more ready for this right now is…'

Josh put his hand to his mouth, waiting for her answer. It was the tensest moment of all their lives. If Nicole sent their rivals home too, they would automatically be through to the next round.

'…Union J! The act I'm sending home is District 3.'

They couldn't believe it. Jumping up and down and hugging each other, their nerves disappeared completely, replaced by a huge feeling of happiness. Even if they were voted out next week – which they hoped wouldn't happen – they had won the battle of the boy bands. But when District 3 trudged over to give them all hugs, suddenly they felt sad again. Their friends were going home because of them.

That night, on *The Xtra Factor*, a caller asked Nicole whether she thought Union J would make the final – after all, they'd now been in the bottom two twice.

'Anything is possible,' she said, brightly. 'Imagine where Union J started and how far they've come already, they've grown so much! Lord knows they've got a lot of fans.'

The audience cheered when she added: 'I can barely get my car in every day because there's so many Union J fans waiting outside. All it takes is believers and they have a lot of believers.'

Dermot O'Leary had also seen the thousands of fans outside the *X Factor* studios. 'Whenever I turn up to soundcheck there's always hundreds of fans outside and I ask who they're voting for, and every single one says District 3 or Union J.'

He'd been astonished that they were both in the bottom two that night – both their Saturday night performances had been amazing.

The Union J boys spoke to Caroline Flack and Olly Murs about what it had felt like to sing off against District 3.

'We kind of knew it was coming,' said Josh. 'We spoke to District 3 and we said, "Can you imagine?" Perhaps we shouldn't have said anything.'

Jaymi was very emotional. 'It was gutting, getting through and we were like, breaking down, 'cause that's like our best mates. It's such mixed emotions.'

And he chatted about the rivalry between the two bands, saying: 'There's a healthy rivalry but we've become best of mates. It was hard enough singing against Jade and seeing her go out, but this was a million times harder because they want it just as much as us and you've got a bond 'cause you're both in groups, so you both know what it feels like.'

Then the presenters decided to lighten the mood. It had been a sad day and everyone needed a bit of cheering up. And nothing cheers people up better than an embarrassing revelation!

'We've heard that you, Josh, are wearing boxer shorts that say "Believe The Hype" on them. Is this true?' asked Caroline Flack, giggling.

Everyone laughed and of course Josh had to pull his jeans down to show everyone. He went bright red!

Little Mix said neither of the bands deserved to be in the bottom two – and then admitted to fancying the Union J boys!

On the weekly segment, 'Fighting Talk', George and Ella battled it out in a fake boxing ring, starting more rumours that they were secretly dating.

'Ella's going down!' said George playfully, as they got ready to start the war of words.

Question one: How many relationships have you had?

Ella admitted she'd had none, while George bragged that he had ten!

'He's never even had a girlfriend,' joked Ella.

Question two: How many schools have you attended?

Ella said two, while George said seven.

'Did you get kicked out of loads?' asked Ella.

'No,' replied George, giving her his cheekiest smile. 'I'm an international jet-setter.' It wasn't true at all!

Clearly the pair had great chemistry as they joked around, answering the silly questions.

Question three: how many animals have you had?

Ella said she'd had about seventeen pets and listed them all – bunnies, parrots, ducks, geese, fish – the list was endless.

George was obviously feeling very left out.

'I've had a giraffe, an elephant and a lion,' he lied. But this was all in good humour and everyone found it very funny.

That night, the boys went back to their hotel for a well-earned rest. Union J were safe for another week but it had been an epic night, one they would never forget. And with their main rivals out of the competition they were in a strong position to go far. But first they had to say goodbye to Greg, Dan and Mickey and that can't have been easy, especially when they knew they were the reason the trio were leaving.

The boys went to bed feeling a mixture of happiness and sadness but as Dermot O'Leary had said: 'District 3 have sung their last song in this competition, but the other acts must go on.'

CHAPTER ELEVEN

PERFORMANCE IN PARIS

WEEK SEVEN ~ GUILTY PLEASURES
17/18 November 2012

What Union J sang: 'Call Me Maybe' – Carly Rae Jepsen

What the judges said:
Tulisa: 'I'm not a fan of that song.'
Gary: 'I think you've definitely bounced back from last week.'
Nicole: 'You sounded really, really good.'
Louis: 'You can't be in the bottom two again.'

It was dark and the night had a chill to it, as a young couple took a midnight stroll in November, hand in hand through the West End of London. She was dressed in a cosy coat, her long hair flowing, while he was covering his curly locks with a wooly hat. Holding hands, they looked like any other young couple as they walked back to the hotel they were staying in.

But onlookers were stunned to see that it was Ella Henderson and George Shelley – were all the rumours true? Were they an item?

It was just a few days before that Ella had protested they were not boyfriend and girlfriend and had spoken about how they were just friends. She told *Fabulous* magazine: 'We've got a lot in common, we're in synch with one another. You don't come into this competition or this kind of show to make a friend for life and stuff, but with certain people I think I've found that.'

But clutching each other's hands on the cold evening, passers-by saw a completely different story.

Wrapping up warm, all the boys were remarkably bright-eyed as they arrived the next day at King's Cross St Pancras station. After finishing in the bottom two the week before, they knew they had a lot of work to do to get their confidence back up. Plus, it had been a sad time for the foursome. Saying goodbye to their friends in District 3 had been tough, especially since they were the ones who were chosen to continue in the competition – over their mates Greg, Dan and Mickey. But they were grinning ear to ear when they were handed a glass of champagne, before stepping onto the Eurostar train.

The boys and the remaining finalists were all off to Disneyland, Paris!

'You'll be performing for their 20th Anniversary,' Louis had told them, watching their eyes light up. It was to be their first performance away from the *X Factor* stage and naturally it was a very big deal.

For the boys it was their first real step on the road to being a proper band. They would be entertaining thousands of people and not all of them would even have heard of Union J. Their job was to convert them into fans!

Unable to contain his excitement, Josh tweeted: 'WE ARE OFF TO DISNEYLAND PARIS!!!!!! Ah...soooo exciting!! I can't wait to go on the flying dumbo ride!!'

They were so excited, in fact, that according to the *Daily Mirror* they spent the whole of the journey drawing moustaches on Christopher Maloney's face as he slept.

But before their stage time, the boys got to enjoy the theme park. Greeted by Disney royalty Mickey and Minnie, all the finalists swarmed around the famous mice. But Ella was definitely Mickey's favourite – he threw his arms around her as soon as he saw her. Wearing a fun blue spotty skirt with some Minnie ears, they looked like the perfect couple – we hope George wasn't jealous!

But in fact George had the biggest grin of everyone as the finalists took in the sights, munched on French treats and were completely mobbed by autograph hunters.

The guys were so surprised. Being far away from England, they didn't think they'd be recognised but it made them realise just how much of a stir they were making all over the world.

Ella and George posed for photos wearing matching Mickey and Minnie Mouse ears and huge grins – before sharing them on Twitter for their delighted fans.

Disneyland is always exciting and the boys were totally swept away by the lights, the costumes and of course the rides. Ella joined them on the log flume and screamed with laughter as it whisked the finalists around the park.

Excitable George went on rollercoaster after rollercoaster, including one he tried out with presenter Caroline Flack. He went on the Space Mountain ride with her too, along with fellow finalist Jahmene. But after a few hours, he began to look pale.

It was soon obvious something was wrong – he wasn't his usual self at all. Eventually he gave his bandmates some distressing news: he'd overdone it and needed to lie down!

So while Jaymi, Josh and JJ continued to enjoy themselves with the rest of the finalists, poor George went back to his hotel and tried to sleep his nausea off. All that up and down and round and round will do that to you, George!

It was obvious he'd learnt his lesson, but would he be okay for their first ever, proper performance that evening?

The boys were a bit worried as they wandered around, enjoying everything the park had to offer.

George stayed in bed, missing out on the fun. He must have been feeling very sorry for himself; he was desperate to be well enough for his first ever live performance outside of *X Factor*. All he could do was hope.

But while George was laid low, the other finalists were surprised to see his rumoured love, Ella, getting very close to his bandmate Josh Cuthbert.

It was him she sat next to on the rides, laughing and screaming with joy. Onlookers were left to wonder if maybe Ella had stayed tight-lipped about her romance with George because her feelings were shifting towards his friend and co-singer.

One eagle-eyed fan even told the *Daily Mirror* that they had seen Ella and Josh walking back to the *X Factor* hotel earlier in the week, with their arms around each other. Another source told the paper that George was so devastated that he was on the verge of tears when he found out about the walk – and that Rylan had to calm him down.

George had only just revealed to *The X Factor* online that he would consider dating the songstress once the show was over.

So, would the boys battle over Ella?

Only time would tell.

DID YOU KNOW?

Melanie Masson runs a music class for under-fives called Fairy Flutterby's Little Rockabyes – so Melanie is known as 'Fairy Flutterby'!

At the eleventh hour, George declared that he was well enough to perform, much to everyone's relief.

As day turned to night, the Disneyland stage was set for a magical show. A huge glittering white Christmas tree nestled on huge blocks of snow, providing the backdrop for the impending performances. Placed directly in front of the famous Disney castle, which was lit up in purple, it looked like something out of a fairytale.

In the contestants' rooms the mood was frantic but everyone was in high spirits. Outfits were chosen and put on, hair styled and re-styled, make-up carefully applied. The excitement was palpable – just a few months before they were at school or stacking shelves. They must have felt as if they were living in their own Disney movie – a rags-to-riches tale every bit as romantic as *Cinderella*.

First onto the winter-themed stage was Rylan Clark, dressed for once in a smart outfit of tight black jeans, white open T-shirt and black blazer. He even seemed a little stage-struck as he belted out a Spice Girls medley in front of the 1,200 people in the audience. But he energetically stormed the stage, screaming: 'Alright, Disney, I think we need to have a bit of fun tonight. I love the Spice Girls! Cheers, Disney – see you later!'

Next up were our favourite boys, Union J, in coordinated brown jackets and dark jeans. Waving to the hordes of fans they put their heart and soul into singing Leona Lewis' 'Bleeding Love'. The audience was overwhelmed by the foursome, who were now experiencing the adulation of a top-selling stadium band. And the feeling was reciprocated, with George telling them: 'Thank you so much, that's the first time we have performed outside *The X Factor* so it's such an amazing feeling!'

Next to experience the excitement of the lucky crowds was Ella Henderson, who had kept her Minnie Mouse ears on, teaming them with matching gloves. Much to everyone's delight, she chose to sing the Katy Perry classic, 'Firework'. It must have been an amazing feeling to hear so many people singing along to the well-known tune with her.

It was a perfect song. As the stage lights flickered and changed through a rainbow of colours, Ella looked right at home in Disneyland. She told the crowds: 'It has been amazing! I have loved it here. It's like being in a fairytale!'

DID YOU KNOW?

Ella has always been a huge Minnie Mouse fan and was so excited to meet her – along with her other Disney favourites, Cinderella and Ariel.

Somewhat surprisingly, Christopher Maloney was the only finalist to sing a Disney song, choosing 'A Whole New World' from *Aladdin*. 'Can I just say, ladies and gentlemen, boys and girls,' he said humbly, 'giving me this opportunity to sing today has been amazing. If you had told me ten months ago that I would be singing at Disney, in front of the castle, to celebrate their 20th Anniversary, I really wouldn't have believed it. Thank you so much for all your amazing support.'

As the final contestant left the stage, the crowds must have been feeling a little deflated but then Caroline Flack appeared and told them: 'We've had the most amazing day here, so thank you so much.'

They began to cheer with delight as the *X Factor* stars trooped back on stage – accompanied by their favourite Disney stars!

Jahmene was with Donald Duck and James Arthur was with Goofy – although Rylan, whose actual companion was Pluto – stole him away for a huge hug. Christopher Maloney had main star Mickey by his side, while Ella obviously was holding hands with her beloved Minnie. Union J had the cheeky Chipmunks to contend with, all dressed in Santa outfits.

After their exciting time in Paris, the contestants flew back and began to prepare for Saturday night's show – Guilty Pleasures.

The singers had to pick their own embarrassing guilty song pleasure, and reinvent it to make it cool again. But our favourite bandmates found the time to support one of their favourite charities first – by trying to get all their fans to support them, too. They tweeted: 'Everyone please check out an amazing charity for children with brain tumours. They are amazing and so lovely @JossSearchlight RT RT josh xxx'.

It just proved how lovely all the boys are. They were thinking of other people even when they had so much work to do.

With fewer and fewer girls left in the competition, the *X Factor* styling team may have been feeling disappointed that they didn't have as much make-up to apply to the contestants' faces but in a series of photos on Facebook, it was revealed that the make-up team were still being kept busy – because the boys from Union J also wear eyeliner and foundation to go on stage!

Josh was photographed having mascara added to his eyelashes, while George was being primped and preened by the hairdressing team. And George had some explaining to do when he was seen with a bright red lipstick mark on his cheek… care of an over-enthusiastic fan outside the studio!

DID YOU KNOW?

District 3 is also the name of one of the fictional colonies in *The Hunger Games.*

With three weeks to go, the mood backstage at the *X Factor* arena was tense. As the seats began to fill up, it was clear that this would be another packed live show.

'Six acts remain but none of them can take anything for granted,' announced Dermot O'Leary, as the live show began. Trying to relax the nervous crowd, he asked the judges about their own guilty pleasure songs.

Nicole replied: '"Push It" by Salt-n-Pepa.'

Gary said: 'Anything by Rick Astley.'

Tulisa revealed: 'The Backstreet Boys.'

And Louis really showed his age when he said: 'Engelbert Humperdinck', before changing his mind to 'Take That' after seeing Dermot's embarrassed face.

Earlier on in the week, Louis had given the boys a pep talk to try and give them a much-needed boost.

'Guys, it was really tough,' he told them. 'It was the battle of the boy bands. You're going to have to work really hard.'

The boys nodded enthusiastically in reply, and Josh said:

'Last week was really devastating for us to be in the bottom two. It was really hard going up against some of our best mates in the competition.'

After the devastating showdown, Ella had run up to them and said that she was worried she was going to lose her four big brothers!

After their mentor had given them his vote of confidence, the boys felt much better. 'We're coming back fighting! Kerpow!' they yelled.

When they bounced onto the stage, it was with a renewed enthusiasm. They had the audience clapping as they sang the hit song 'Call Me Maybe' to cheers of excitement. Smiling and obviously enjoying themselves, the song went down a storm with both fans at home and in the crowd. But it was the judges' verdict that mattered, and that must have been all they could think about when they finished singing.

The cheers hadn't even died down when Tulisa began to speak. 'Guys,' she began sadly, 'I'm going to be really honest…' It was obvious that she wasn't happy, and the crowd began to boo. 'This is a really hard performance for me to judge and I'll tell you why: I'm not a big fan of that song.'

As the booing got louder, Tulisa was quick to say, 'I think you sounded great – it had good energy. But it's still too cheesy for me and the whole point of guilty pleasures is to take a cheesy song and make it cool – maybe there wasn't enough of that for me.'

The boys looked crestfallen, and even Gary appeared shocked by Tulisa's comments but he came to the boys' defence immediately, saying, 'If it's guilty to like that song, then I love it! It's been one of the best songs of the year and I think you've never looked better.'

Shadow Chancellor Ed Balls was watching at home and tweeted his disagreement, too! 'Sorry Tulisa,' it read. 'But Carly Rae Jepsen's "Call Me Maybe" was THE song of 2012'!

Their spirits definitely began to soar as Gary continued: 'I think so far for you guys you've always been competing with the other band – and now you've won the battle of the boy bands, it's about winning for you guys.'

The icing on the cake was when he finished with: 'You know what? That was a pretty good performance from you tonight, I think you've definitely bounced back from last week.'

And things only got better when Nicole told them that she thought the boys had done the song justice. She'd spotted the audience drooling over the good-looking guys and had some advice for the group.

'Engage with the audience more,' she said, wisely. 'What I would like to see from you is to get a little bit more creative with your staging. Enjoy it, love it – and you look expensive and that counts, too!'

The boys had certainly come a long way since they'd arrived wearing nothing but their fresh faces and high street clothes to the London audition. And to have Nicole recognise this was amazing.

Dermot spoke about the hordes of swooning fans that had begun to follow them everywhere. The boys chuckled as he said: 'You turn up for rehearsals there are loads of girls outside, all chanting your name. The girls down the front, they all love Union J. You've been in the bottom two twice – what is it, Louis?'

Louis looked just as puzzled as Dermot as he tried to think what could possibly have led to the sing-off. Totally stumped, all he could say was that he still truly believed Union J would be the next big boy band.

George had obviously thought long and hard about what could have been letting them down. The whole band knew they had something special, they believed in themselves, just as the thousands of fans they had accumulated since that first moment when they appeared on TV at the auditions.

'I think it was quite difficult to have the two boy bands and the rivalry, and maybe votes were being split between the two,' he mused. 'But we just wanted to come back fighting this week and we tried really, really hard.'

It was the kind of observation that showed a wisdom far beyond his years and in homes all over the country, people were nodding in agreement.

DID YOU KNOW?

Josh's favourite dessert is apple pie, while George likes to get his caffeine fix from Costa Coffee and he also loves home-cooked roast dinners. Get your aprons on, girls!

It was an evening of outstanding talent and all the contestants who followed Union J's opening performance really sang their hearts out.

After an anxious night's sleep, the six final acts returned to the *X Factor* studios to hear their fate but they were about to receive what has been described as the biggest shock in the show's history. That night, the contestants all performed Tulisa's song, 'Young', before *X Factor* alumni Olly Murs and R&B superstar Alicia Keys each took to the stage to entertain the crowds. They certainly showed the finalists how to perform like pros! As the live camera watched their every move, it was then time for the quarter-finalists to be announced.

Chris Maloney mouthed to his family: 'I'm going home,' before the jaw-dropping results were revealed. It was a relief when Union J quickly learnt that they were safe for another week. But the sing-off would be between James Arthur and Ella Henderson!

The boys' hearts must have skipped a few beats. They were through to the quarterfinals of *X Factor* 2012! But the moment was bittersweet – their beloved Ella wasn't safe from elimination. She could be going home.

Dermot O'Leary couldn't hide his surprise. To him, as to people all around the UK, it was unbelievable that one of those two acts would be going home.

Leona Lewis tweeted: 'No way should Ella and James be singing against each other.'

A wave of anger swept the nation – but the worst was yet to come. Union J nervously went backstage to wait for the result. Whatever happened, it would be a sad night in the *X Factor* hotel.

After walking out together, arm in arm, both Ella and James took to the stage once more. James performed an acoustic version of Alicia Keys' 'Fallin' on his guitar, while Ella sang Daniel Bedingfield's 'If You're Not The One'.

It was all down to the judges...

Nicole chose to save her singer, James, while Tulisa did the same with her girl, Ella. It was only natural that the judges would save their own acts.

'I shouldn't have to make this decision,' Tulisa lamented, while Nicole tried to ease her guilt by saying that she had no worries about Ella's career, but she had to stick with 'her boy'. Now it was down to Gary and Louis – what would they decide?

Louis went first, saying: 'I'm in shock – I thought they were two finalists. Nicole and Tulisa are broken-hearted. Ella, you have so much potential. You've got so much more to give in this competition. James, you are amazing. You're a readymade act for a record deal...'

Then he made his decision: 'But the act I'm sending home is James.'

Gary was quiet for a moment before he announced his decision. 'It's about the vocals,' he finally said. 'It's a singing competition. The act I'm sending home is Ella.'

Everyone was stunned.

It was a deadlock, which meant it would all come down to the public vote. And when it was revealed that James Arthur had more votes than Ella Henderson, the audience went into a stunned silence before erupting with anger.

Ella – the nation's newest sweetheart – was going home!

Being the sweet and talented teen she is, Ella graciously accepted her fate. Standing beside a visibly pained Tulisa, she took her last moments on stage to thank and praise her fellow contestants.

'I've grown so much as a person,' she said, full of emotion, 'and that's what I'm taking with me.'

Meanwhile, on Twitter and Facebook angry fans vented their rage. *TOWIE's* Arg wrote: 'Can't believe @Ella_Henderson gone! She deserved to be in the final and more.' While fellow reality star Millie Mackintosh asked: 'How did @Ella_Henderson just get voted out?' And teen starlet Chloë Grace Moretz, of *Kick Ass* fame, was so upset she decided to boycott the show, saying: 'Not watching #XFactorUK anymore. Such a rig.'

It's a wonder the *X Factor* judges weren't a teensy bit afraid – after all, Chloë knows a lot about martial arts!

But Union J were the most devastated at the loss of the

pretty teen. Whatever the rumours of romance that had been flying around, there was no denying how close the boys were to their fellow contestant. And if there was any bad feeling between George and Josh, it was put to one side while they shared their sorrow at her loss.

Tears rolled down their cheeks as Ella left the stage to thunderous applause for the last time. And it was to the Union J boys that she went first, where she was cocooned in hugs.

'We've lost one of the most amazing people in the world,' Josh told Caroline Flack, after the showdown.

Selflessly, the boys refused to wallow in their own misery. Instead they decided to cheer Ella up by taking her back to the hotel they all shared and plying her with sweet treats.

'I was with them at the hotel last night,' Ella told *Metro* the following day. 'It's a horrible feeling but I'll be seeing them soon and hopefully I'll be seeing them there, singing at the final.'

Naming her the band's unofficial fifth member, Union J tweeted: 'Gutted for @ella_henderson but she will be massive anyway!! She's amazing!!'

Although they'd already said that *X Factor* hairdresser Jamie Stevens should be their fifth member, who knows how big the band will grow? It's nice to know they've got such huge hearts.

DID YOU KNOW?

Lucy Spraggan has 'Olly Murs' tattooed on her right foot. She asked the presenter/singer to perform with her on *The Xtra Factor* and in exchange she said she'd have his name inked – she kept her word!

The following morning Ella was up bright and early. She had an interview to give with Phillip Schofield and Holly Willoughby on ITV's *This Morning* and she took the opportunity to show her support for her favourite finalists, Union J.

'I'm definitely going to be supporting Union J,' she said, confidently. 'They're like my big brothers.'

She also revealed she had a gut feeling that she was going to be eliminated, even though she said that she felt more in control of her performance that night than ever.

'Everyone assumed that I'd go through to the final but so much good stuff is going to come off the back of this for me,' she told the presenters.

No one doubted it.

CHAPTER TWELVE

KNUCKLING DOWN

WEEK EIGHT ~ ABBA VS MOTOWN
24/25 November 2012

What Union J sang: 'The Winner Takes It All' – ABBA/'I'll Be There' – Jackson Five

What the judges said:
Tulisa: 'What a night for you guys!'
Gary: 'I think you're on a roll now.'
Nicole: 'I felt like I was watching your concert.'
Louis: 'I think the next big boy band is on stage.'

Emotions were already high in the *X Factor* hotel. The final was drawing near and everyone was fretting over what they could do to make their act the winning one. But one contestant was struggling more than most, and his worries had nothing to do with the weekend's drama.

A young fan had asked him a question and he didn't know how to answer it.

Jaymi Hensley went to his mentor, Louis Walsh, to talk it through. And with his help he came to a decision: it was time to tell the world he was gay.

The heartthrob wasn't the only gay finalist in the show – Rylan Clark, Lucy Spraggan and Jade Ellis had all proudly admitted their sexuality. And he didn't want to hide it to gain votes, because Jaymi is very proud of who he is but for one reason or another, he had decided to keep it to himself.

Now it was time to tell the world.

His bandmates had always known the truth: that he had been in a relationship with his boyfriend, a hairdresser, for three years. Totally loved-up, the couple planned to marry and have children.

'I didn't want to do it in five years' time when I have a career,' he told the *Sun On Sunday*. 'I don't think anyone should have to hide who they are.'

The *X Factor* bosses and of course, Jaymi's mentor Louis (who is also gay) were a real help in his decision. 'If I can help just one kid out, that's enough for me,' said Louis. He even laughed and added: 'Every boy band has got to have a gay one!'

Jaymi's bandmates publicly rallied round in support of his bold move. 'It's been a tough week but we're so proud of Jaymi. He's so brave,' they told the *Metro*. 'It will help out other people having a tough time and give them courage.'

Jaymi and the band were really thrilled with the support they received from their fans who overwhelmed them with positive tweets.

A few days later they all wrapped up warm and attended the opening night party of 'Winter Wonderland' in London's Hyde Park. With fake snow, fun rides and lots of Christmassy music it was a great night but they couldn't enjoy themselves too much because this week they had to sing two songs at the live show, which would be the quarterfinals.

They would have to learn one ABBA song and one Motown classic. It was twice as much work and with the final just around the corner, they didn't want to let themselves or Louis down, especially now they were so close to winning.

Gary Barlow managed to take some time out that week, too – to collect his OBE! He was invited to Buckingham Palace to meet HM the Queen, who thanked him for his Services to Charity and the Entertainment Industry and pinned the award on his chest. Such an honour!

DID YOU KNOW?

Rylan Clark was once mugged by a fox! After coming face to face with the creature one evening, he was so surprised that he dropped his wallet – which Foxy picked up and ran away with.

That week the boys were very excited about their performance. Rehearsals had gone well and they knew every note of their songs. They also thought they sounded really good and couldn't wait to show off on stage!

At the live show, it was finally their turn to sing. The stage was empty except for the four boys, as they began their first performance of the night.

Josh began to sing 'The Winner Takes It All' and the boys must have been hoping that the lyrics would come true! Of course they wanted to be the winners and to take it all – 'all' being a recording contract and a long career as a band. They moved over to the audience and took the hands of a few lucky fans as they sang.

And Tulisa was grinning as they finished their first song of the night. 'You know what, guys? I've got to give it to you – the vocals were on point tonight, with Jaymi really taking the lead there,' she began. 'The staging was simple, no gimmicks, just you and the voice. Good job, Louis – I really loved that!'

It had started well, but what would grumpy Gary say?

'Guys, I feel so good about this band, it just feels right,' he said, heaping more praise onto the happy boys. 'Like Tulisa said, you sounded great tonight and you look great tonight.'

No one was going to argue with that – the boys looked hotter than ever. 'Josh, your voice is coming through as well – I thought that was particularly good from you,' he added, singling Josh out. 'I think you're on a roll now, guys, I really do.'

Wow! It was high praise indeed from the normally serious judge.

Then it was Nicole's turn to speak and the boys were hoping she'd agree with Gary and Tulisa – to get great comments from all the judges on one night would be just amazing.

'Boys,' she said in her sexiest voice. 'I love the way you addressed the girls this week – get used to it, get comfortable with it 'cause that's what your future looks like, right up on that stage. I felt like I was watching your concert.'

She was totally right. It had felt like a real concert for the boys and for the first time they must have felt this week was almost in the bag.

Nicole also commented on Josh's great voice, saying: 'Josh, you have such a beautiful voice and whenever you sing, you sing with such ease.'

All they could do was thank the stunning brunette.

As usual, Louis was brimming with pride: 'Yes, Josh and Jaymi did the lead vocals, but the four guys sing, everybody sings in this band and they work so hard.'

It was obvious how far they'd all come from that first week when they'd been told off for not working hard enough. The boys had really knuckled down and their efforts were definitely paying off. They looked as if they couldn't wait to get off stage and jump around, screaming for joy.

But Louis took a moment to beg the public to vote for his boys. Ella's recent shock departure had made it very clear that however much everyone might like an act, they would leave the stage if people didn't pick up the phone.

No one wanted that to happen.

On stage, George was so happy he couldn't speak. But even as they walked off the boys knew that tonight wasn't over – they had one more song to sing and it had to be good for them to reach the grand final, now just two weeks away.

They couldn't relax, but they waited patiently for the other five acts to sing their songs before it was once more their turn. This time Jaymi kicked off proceedings with the Jackson Five classic 'I'll Be There' – and he sounded brilliant! It sounded so polished and George looked particularly fit. He was really turning into a hunk on stage and the girls all loved him. That kind of adoration is a lot for a teenager to take, but George looked perfectly at ease with it, and wasn't distracted when he heard his name being shouted out from the audience, over and over.

All they could do now was listen as the judges said what they thought of their second song.

'Wow, guys, what a night for you!' said Tulisa, blown away by the band. 'Two amazing song choices, two amazing vocal performances! For me this is your best night in the competition.'

It was just what they wanted to hear – they'd nailed it!

But Gary had returned to his former grumpy self. Obviously one heap of praise was enough for one night. 'What you had tonight with Motown was a massive opportunity. Boy bands were essentially born in the Motown era – The Drifters, The Temptations, The Four Tops…'

Already people were yawning as Gary droned on.

'I thought that was an open door for you guys to do something really one-off tonight and you didn't really take that opportunity.'

No one agreed with him. Anywhere. But still he kept going.

'It was a good performance,' he admitted, 'but I thought you could have gone the extra mile there and you didn't.'

What was he expecting? Fireworks? Gymnastics?

The judges began to argue among themselves. 'It was a great performance,' insisted Tulisa, backed up by Louis. And Nicole added: 'I think all the little girls will beg to differ right now. Because they will pretty much be playing it on repeat.'

All the little girls – and all the big ones! Everyone loved the boys and no one could understand why Gary was being so negative.

'Guys, that was your best performance yet,' pronounced Louis, after asking if Gary had recently gone deaf. 'That was amazing! We didn't want to play it safe; we took a chance. These boys are a vocal harmony band and they've got something special.'

And with that, the audience erupted into cheers again.

Jaymi leapt to the defence of his bandmates: 'The reason we've kept it safe is that we've really found out who we are as a band on this show. We've learnt every week who we are and where our market is, and we just wanted to show that we could take a song and make it a Union J song.'

All the boys nodded because that was exactly what they had done. But was it enough to get them through to the semi-finals?

Thousands of their fans certainly thought so – including Little Mix, who tweeted: 'Union j's best performance last night smashed it make sure you vote for them guys nobody is safe.' And Niall Horan from One Direction was pretty impressed, too, tweeting: '@UnionJworld congrats lads! Smashed it tonight! Great job! Proud!'

Before they went to sleep, the boys took some time to say goodnight to their fans: 'Off to bed now sooo tired had a wicked night tho thanks so much for your support and if you have already voted. We love you all nite JJx.'

DID YOU KNOW?

James Arthur once wet the bed on a family holiday – after drinking too many ginger beers. Aw!

The next day, the boys were a bag of nerves but they still tried to have some fun. George posted a really cute picture of Josh, fast asleep, sucking his thumb, before they all spent some time with their fans, chatting and signing autographs and having pictures taken.

There were so many fans, though, and so little time!

They spent most of the day rehearsing their 'save me' song for that night, although they were all hoping they wouldn't have to sing it. Then it was time for Dermot O'Leary to leap on stage and announce the start of *The X Factor Results Show*.

The acts watched as Bruno Mars sang his new track, 'Locked Out Of Heaven', before superstar Rihanna performed 'Diamonds' on the stage, as a shower of rain gently fell on her from above. By the end of the performance she was soaking wet, but she still looked gorgeous!

After all the excitement, it was time for Dermot to deliver the good and bad news – it was time for the results.

'The first act through is…' he began. 'James Arthur!'

The tension on stage was unbearable and everyone clung to each other in solidarity.

'…then Christopher Maloney!'

Dermot paused. There were three acts left, but only one more would be safe. The audience scanned the stage, wondering who would be in the sing-off. Jahmene and Union J had both given brilliant performances, and Rylan had been his usual entertaining self – who would be the third and final act through to safety?

'The final act through to the semi-finals next week is…'

There was a long and dramatic pause.

'…Jahmene!'

Everyone was completely astonished – Union J were in the bottom two again. And this time they would be singing against Essex favourite Rylan. Whoever went, there would be thousands of devastated fans across the country that night. But first, the two downhearted acts would have to pick up their spirits and sing again for the judges.

Rylan went first, performing a slow and emotional version of Athlete's hit, 'Wires'. Vocally, it was his best performance of the season. There were no gimmicks, no dancing – just Rylan, full of emotion, singing for his safety. But it was bad news for the Union J boys – they could see that it was an amazing performance. Then, while Rylan hugged Dermot at the side of the stage, it was time for the boys to give it their all, singing Snow Patrol's 'Run'.

The pain was clearly etched on their faces as they belted out the track. It was a phenomenal performance with JJ, Josh, George and Jaymi giving it everything they had. This was the third time they had been in the bottom two – would they survive again?

When they had finished, Rylan and Dermot joined them on stage to face the judges.

Nicole went first. 'Boys, that was a very moving performance,' she told Union J. 'Thank you so much – it was passionate, it was emotional, but it is simple for me. I have to stick with my boy, I believe in him – the act I'm sending home is Union J.'

The boys clapped – they didn't expect anything else. Nicole was Rylan's mentor, and very loyal. Of course she would save him.

Next went Louis, who gave the boys a huge smile. 'Rylan, you're a fantastic guy. You're brilliant fun, you're a great role model, you're a team player, and you're a brilliant performer,' he began. Nobody disagreed with him. 'And I've enjoyed meeting you, and working with you and talking to you – I think you're going to have an amazing career in television and everything.'

Rylan smiled. He knew what was coming next.

'But Dermot, in the sing-off, the boys totally won. As Tulisa would say, they nailed it. The act I'm sending home is Rylan.'

One vote apiece and now it was Gary's turn. The judge had never pretended to like Rylan's act before, but anything could happen.

'Union J, you had a great night last night and also you've just had a great sing-off as well – you're the band every-one is going to want to sign in this competition. You're going to have the labels fighting over you. Well done on that performance.'

The audience began to chant: 'Union J, Union J, Union J…'

'Listen, Rylan,' Gary said softly. 'You have been an amazing contestant and I'm so glad, because tonight that was your best vocal performance and also, your best song choice – that was one of my favourite songs.'

It was good to hear something nice about Rylan coming from Barlow – but would he go so far as to save him over Union J?

'We've had great fun, none of it has been personal – we've not taken any of it off the stage,' he added.

Rylan totally agreed – he was really happy. Gary was finally making up with him after weeks of slating his performances.

'But the act I'm sending home tonight, I'm sad to say, is Rylan.'

So, it was down to Tulisa – she would have the deciding vote. It was a horrible position to be in, but a decision had to be made.

'Union J, you are four amazing lads – on stage and off stage, and you've given brilliant performances each week,' she said. 'Rylan, you have entertained me the whole of this series. You've made me laugh, you've made me smile, and I have to admire your strength for some of the stuff you've had to put up with, while being in this competition…'

It was time for her to cast her vote.

'Now at this stage I have to go with the act that I feel has the most potential to sell records in this competition. I'm so sorry, it pains me to say this, but the act I'm sending home is Rylan.'

The sick feeling in the boys' tummies went away and

they were left overwhelmed with happiness. They'd made it to the semi-finals! Now they were one step closer to winning *The X Factor*.

Rylan congratulated the boys, who were once again left feeling very guilty. They hated seeing their friends leave the competition, especially when they had been picked over them. But when they left the stage they tweeted: 'We certainly know how it feels to be in the bottom 2! We just wanna make it through to the final now. Thank you to everyone who voted.'

And Sharon Osbourne, who had helped Louis put the boys through in Vegas, was pleased too, tweeting: 'Congratulations to Union J. Well done boys! Big Kiss, Mrs O.'

DID YOU KNOW?

Jade Ellis dated Marvin Humes from JLS when she was fifteen. They met when they both entered a local talent competition in Southeast London.

On *The Xtra Factor*, Rylan told Caroline Flack and Olly Murs that he was relieved. 'I feel like a weight's been lifted off my shoulders, like I've been let out of prison!' The presenters laughed as he went on: 'Not in a bad way, I've loved being here – you know what I mean.' Then he said he'd miss Gary, describing him as being like the uncle he never wanted but loved anyway. Gary laughed. The two had definitely buried the hatchet.

Later on, Caroline congratulated the Union J boys on getting through to the semi-finals and Josh said: 'It's quite sad, really – we're chuffed to be here but it's bittersweet to see Rylan go. It was weird being in the bottom two again.'

The boys said they weren't surprised to be in the bottom

two because the quality of the other acts was so good. But Jaymi added: 'I think it's going to give us the fight to go all the way, because every time we've been in the bottom two we've really used it.'

JJ revealed he had a tattoo of a heart on his bum before he took the opportunity to tell everyone that the messiest person in the group was Josh, because he had so many clothes.

'Josh has got a ridiculous amount of clothes,' he said. 'I've never seen so many.'

Josh said that Jaymi was the biggest prankster of the group, but they all wound up JJ the most and pulled pranks on him all the time. Poor JJ…

After getting through to the semi-final, James Arthur was so excited that he immediately went out to celebrate at Whisky Mist. When he left – much later on in the night – he had lipstick smeared all over his face! He was definitely being tipped to win the show – could Union J beat him? They could only try…

Before they went to bed, the boys had time for one last tweet: 'Off to sleep ;) going to miss rylan an awful lot…he's such an amazing guy inside and out. Friend for life :) night night josh xx'.

DID YOU KNOW?

Union J's Josh would have David Beckham, Rita Ora and Caroline Flack as his ideal dinner guests.

CHAPTER THIRTEEN

A NATION DIVIDED

WEEK NINE ~ SONGS FOR YOU
1/2 December 2012

What Union J sang: 'Beneath Your Beautiful' – Emeli Sandé and Labrinth/'I'm Already There' – Lonestar

What the judges said:

Tulisa: 'It felt like a really mature performance.'
Gary: 'Good vocals, nice song choice.'
Nicole: 'I loved it – you've grown so much.'
Louis: 'The next big boy band is Union J!'

It had been a shocking weekend for the boys and they now had little time to recover themselves. The semi-finals were less than a week away and they had a lot of work to do.

UNION J AND DISTRICT 3: BATTLE OF THE BANDS

After having to fight their way through yet another sing-off, it was hardly surprising that their spirits were low. Their Saturday night performances had been exceptional and even Louis was convinced that there was no way his boys would be in the bottom two again. In fact, he'd told them exactly that, moments before they discovered they would be singing for their survival for a third time.

After Rylan was sent home, Josh, JJ, Jaymi and George were all exhausted and emotional. Backstage, George even looked close to tears.

'We're too close to give up,' Jaymi said, when the show was over. 'We've now just got to come back fighting.'

He had given the cameras a brave smile, and put his arms around poor George.

But the next morning the boys were up bright and early, and talking to their fans. They tweeted: 'Good morning! SOOO happy we're still here. Sorry if we let you down this week, we're going to try really really hard this week! George X'.

It was straight off to the rehearsal studio for the four talented boys – who were now just two weeks away from the live final.

And when they got to the studio, it was obvious that, after a good night's sleep, they were feeling a bit better.

'You're in the semi-finals!' said Louis, and the boys began to cheer. They had to admit it was a phenomenal achievement in itself, especially against such strong competition.

Louis explained to the boys that this week's theme was 'Songs For You'. They boys could choose any song and dedicate their performance to anyone they wanted. Louis asked: 'Have you any ideas?'

'We were thinking Labrinth and Emeli Sandé,' said Jaymi. '"Beneath Your Beautiful"?'

Louis loved the song choice and immediately agreed.

'We really want to dedicate this song to our fans,' the boys all agreed – and George explained why: 'Our fans have been amazing throughout this competition. Sometimes they get in touch with us and let us know some of the hard times they've been going through,' he said.

'Despite where we are now, we've all have struggles with being picked on in the past, so this song's about being beautiful on the inside, and we really hope people can relate to it at home,' added Jaymi.

Being in the bottom two again had really damaged their confidence and the boys would have to work hard not only on their singing, but also on their morale, to keep their spirits up for the long week ahead.

'Being in the bottom two three times is gutting – knowing that the public aren't voting for you, knowing that we did all we could on Saturday night and gave our best and obviously it wasn't good enough,' said Josh.

But deep down the boys knew it wasn't that simple. The country was being divided and there could only be one winner.

It would be a busy week for Union J – but first their mentor had a surprise for the boys…

Louis had always been confused by his act's obsession with the cosy all-in-one outfits they wore when they were relaxing. 'What's a onesie?' he had asked the boys, after spotting them all wearing them.

George had explained that it was like a baby-grow for adults and Louis had been horrified. He'd told the boys he wouldn't be seen dead in one – unless they got into the semi-finals.

And now here they were, preparing to sing at the semi-finals and the boys hadn't forgotten Louis's words…

'A promise is a promise, so we hope he sticks to it,' Josh told the *X Factor* cameras during rehearsals.

'Louis is more used to wearing suits and turtleneck jumpers,' said George. 'So I don't know how he's going to find wearing a onesie.'

The boys threw themselves into practising on stage for the live show. Then Louis arrived…

'Hey boys, how's it going?' he asked casually. But when they all turned around they were overjoyed to see him wearing a huge green onesie!

'Yes!' they all exclaimed before giving him a huge hug. Louis still looked unsure about the outfit and asked: 'Is it something like Tulisa would wear?'

'You look like a baby,' giggled George as the other boys fell about laughing. 'I'd do anything for you guys,' said Louis. And with their mentor standing in front of them, wearing a giant baby-grow, they truly believed him!

As well as the usual hours practicing and rehearsing, the boys once more got caught up in the never-ending whirlwind of publicity that goes hand in hand with fame and fortune.

First up was a shoot for *Heat* magazine, where they posed for some very sexy new pics, and spoke about how they were amazed at the Union J fever sweeping the country.

'I had a girl faint in my arms on Sunday,' Jaymi told the magazine. 'So I kind of just handed her to a friend!'

It was an emotional week, and everyone was feeling a bit vulnerable. George even told the magazine why he hadn't yet posed for topless pictures.

Despite being a complete dreamboat, he revealed that being bullied in his schooldays had left him less than confident about his body.

'I was obese, I'm massively insecure,' he said. 'I won't even take my top off in the pool. It's programmed into my head that I'm fat because I got bullied at school and I can't get it out. If I got changed for PE and took my top off, people would laugh.'

Poor George – hopefully his new hordes of fans were starting to make him feel a little better.

Meanwhile, Ella Henderson was speaking to the media too. After months of speculation over her love life, she finally revealed that she did fancy one of the Union J boys – and it wasn't George. It was Josh!

'Let me explain it like this,' she told *Look* magazine. 'George Shelley is my best friend. Jaymi Hensley is like my big brother, JJ Hamblett is hilarious…'

But how about Josh – how did she feel about him?

'At the moment it's hard to say,' she said. 'He's still in the competition. As soon as we're both out of it, it's going to go boom…I do want to spend more time with him.'

Hopefully it was the words that Josh had been hoping to hear since meeting the glamorous teen. And it certainly looked that way when he posted a very cute picture of him and Ella together on his Instagram, saying: 'FAVORITE @ellahenderson1!!!!!! :D xx'.

It wasn't long since he'd tweeted: 'Gonna miss you Ella! & I'm gonna miss everything we do togetherrrr!'

Maybe the public was finally getting closer to the truth – that in fact, Ella and Josh could possibly become the *X Factor* couple this year!

Josh wasn't the only Union J boy who had tongues wagging that week either. Devoted JCats all over the country were consumed with jealously when the *Sun* newspaper reported that JJ had a new love – a beautiful Brazilian backing dancer called Rithiely Periera.

She was nicknamed 'Rithy' and according to the tabloid, JJ had met her when she was dancing on *The X Factor*.

When JJ had entered the competition he'd been dating a girl he knew from home. But the pressure of it all had sadly caused them to break up. Were the new rumours true? Was JJ loved up with a backing dancer? Only time would tell...

After five days of rehearsals, the boys got on a plane and flew to Dublin – to appear on the Irish TV series *The Late Late Toy Show*, where they appealed for Ireland to get behind them. 'Louis hasn't won for a few years and we want to do him proud,' Jaymi told the presenters.

They were absolutely overwhelmed by fans from the city – from the moment they got off the plane to the moment they got back on it to fly home. Louis had never seen anything like it and the boys themselves were shocked at the adoration they were inspiring everywhere. They just had to hope that everyone they met would be voting for them at the weekend.

When they arrived back in the UK, it was time for the live show.

It was the semi-final of the competition, and the boys knew how close they were to winning. They would have two songs to sing that night – two chances to get their fans to vote for them – and they were ready to give it their all...

The competition was now between Union J, Jahmene, Christopher Maloney and James Arthur – and all the talented acts wanted to win.

In a shock twist, the judges weren't in control of the boys' fate this week. They could have their say, but it was down to the public at home to decide who would stay and who would go. Who would they vote through to the final in Manchester?

'We're not going down without a fight,' said Josh, back-stage, as he prepared to sing...

Christopher Maloney went first, followed by Jahmene, both giving emotional performances that the judges loved.

Christopher dedicated his to his Gran, who had been the inspiration for him entering the competition in the first place.

Jahmene dedicated his to his brother, who had sadly passed away a few years before.

Then it was time for Union J to give their performance. George strummed on his guitar while the boys stood on stage and sang to their fans. This song was just for them and they wanted each and every one of them to know that they were beautiful, inside and out. It was a lovely sentiment and one that the JCats appreciated.

It was obvious that the boys had really progressed throughout the competition and Tulisa was the first to notice.

Trying to talk over the screams in the audience, she told them: 'I really, really liked that performance. I tell you what, something felt a little bit different about you guys there – it was almost like there's this maturity about you now, it felt like a really mature performance. It's like we've seen you grow over the competition and now you're standing there saying: "We're ready, we wanna be in the final and we're fighting for it".'

Gary was equally happy with the boys and showered praise on them. 'Guys, brilliant performance tonight, what a great song choice. In the past I think you've often sounded like four solo singers in a band but tonight you really blended brilliantly,' he said. 'And you know what, Tulisa's right – there's a calm on stage – you know you're good tonight and it feels really good and I think labels are going to be fighting over you.'

Nicole had only just about got over her tears at Jahmene's emotional performance. But she managed: 'What I love about this group is that you guys are cool, you guys are individual, you're cheese free – a lot of boy groups are cheesy – and Josh, that was a beautiful start to the song. Very honest.'

JJ gave Josh a huge hug – all the boys agreed he'd done them proud that night.

'Everywhere these guys go there's a hysteria,' said Louis. 'You were in Dublin last night – it was like Beatlemania. We've got something great here, guys. JLS came from this. So did One Direction. The next big boy band is Union J!'

Dermot laughed. It was about the hundredth time Louis had said those very words. But surely he was right?

'We respect all of your comments,' said Josh from on stage, 'We're working so hard and we're fingertips away from the final and we want to be there so badly.'

Dermot tried to speak to George next, but as usual, the screams from his fans were too loud. George gave up – and instead of speaking, he shook his head and chuckled, leaving Dermot to thank the boys as they walked off stage.

James Arthur was next and he showed the judges why he was being voted in week after week. He dedicated his song – U2's 'One' – to his brother and sisters, who had always looked up to him. They were getting mobbed every day because of their now famous brother!

Finally, it was time for Union J to sing again. And after Christopher Maloney had received bad feedback following his second performance, they must have thought they now had a very real chance.

Their friends and family raised their Union J signs in the audience, as Louis announced the band back on stage.

For their second song, the boys had wanted to choose a song that symbolised their teamwork with Louis.

They'd gotten really close to their mentor and it was very sweet to dedicate their final song of the night to him – 'I'm Already There', by Lonestar.

This time George sang first and soon the boys was harmonising together beautifully. They sounded stunning.

Whatever happened, the boys must have believed the words they were singing. Even if they didn't win *The X Factor*, they were already where they wanted to be – in the hearts of their fans.

As the music ended and the stage lights found their way back to the judges, the audience began a familiar chant. 'Union J, Union J, Union J…'

The boys huddled together on stage and once more Tulisa was the first to speak. 'Guys, vocally you sounded great tonight, in both performances. But I think you may have played it a little safe with the song choices, because both the songs have been a little bit similar,' she said.

'But at the same time it's about more than just the performances at this stage, it's about all the hard work that you've put in over these past however many weeks and the fight that you've all had. You've been in the bottom two so many times and you're still here, still standing and still fighting and that's the attitude I want to see.'

'Guys, nice performance,' Gary continued. 'Good vocals, nice song choice, but I do agree with Tulisa, it's extremely safe. Are you safe tomorrow night? We can't save you anymore. I think you're at risk now, I really do. But it was a good performance.'

They were sobering words and the boys listened to them with a growing feeling of panic. By the end of his speech,

Gary was fighting to speak over the stream of boos coming from the audience. They certainly didn't agree with the two judges – and neither did Nicole.

'I loved it,' she said. 'You've grown so much and being here tonight in the semi-finals, you are already there…'

Louis begged the people watching at home to vote, before Jaymi said the song they'd chosen may have been safe but it meant a lot to them. 'We miss our families so much,' he added, close to tears. 'We all do,' soothed Dermot, before ushering them off the stage.

And that was it. They boys had done all they could do to secure their place in the final. It was now down to their fans to keep them in the competition…

That night, on *The Xtra Factor*, Caroline and Olly congratulated the boys on their performances, and asked how they were feeling. Josh said: 'No one is safe this week and we're terrified. We're really, really scared.'

Then a caller asked whether the story in the *Sun* about JJ and the backing dancer were true – it was clear that fans all over the country were very worried…

'No, it's not – we're just friends,' he said. 'She's a nice girl but it's not true.'

Phew! So many girls at home must have been heaving huge sighs of relief at the news. Especially when he added: 'I'm still single!'

On Sunday, the boys spent the day preparing for the results show. They practised the song they would sing if they didn't go through, and before they knew it, it was time to head back to the studio. It was nearly time to discover their fate…

The show opened with a great performance by all the acts – accompanied by Rod Stewart! They joined forces to sing 'Merry Christmas, Baby', and all looked like they were having the time of their lives with the megastar. But inside, nerves were eating away at everyone. The waiting was torture. Would Union J make it to the final?

Both Pink and Tulisa took to the stage to perform their new songs for the audience, before it was finally time to find out…

All the acts trooped back on stage. The boys looked very frightened. They desperately wanted to be in the final, even though they had already achieved so much – and would definitely go far whether they won *The X Factor* or not.

They didn't need to win to be successful. Former *X Factor* finalists JLS hadn't won, and neither had One Direction – and both bands were now enjoying mega fame. But the Union J boys had worked so hard and all their fans felt they deserved it…

Walking out with Louis, the boys looked nervous. Their legs must have felt like jelly as they stood with their mentor to hear their fate.

'Okay, it's time for the results,' said Dermot. 'The public have voted and we're about to reveal the three acts going through to next week's final – and the act who received the fewest votes and will be going home tonight…'

The atmosphere was tense, as Dermot wished all the acts the best of luck.

'The first act through to *The X Factor* final is…'

The boys shut their eyes in silent prayer. Christopher looked up to the skies and blinked away tears. Jahmene and James Arthur stared down at the floor.

'…James!'

Hearing his name, James Arthur screamed and nearly collapsed with happiness. Everyone clapped, including the Union J boys.

There were two places left – and three acts hoping to fill them. Who would be next?

'Joining James in the final next week is… Christopher!'

Gary congratulated his act. But Jahmene and Union J could hardly move; they were all so worried.

'Only one more is certain of a place in the final,' said Dermot, speeding up the results. He was conscious that the wait must have been horrible for the two acts left on stage.

'The third and final act through is… Jahmene!'

It was all over.

As Nicole threw her arms around Jahmene, the boys let it sink in: They were going home. They wouldn't be crowned the winners of *The X Factor* 2012.

Struggling to control their emotions, the boys were overwhelmed by hugs from their former fellow contestants.

All the finalists were holding each other so tightly, it was obvious they were all sad to see Union J go. Dermot had to literally drag the boys from their friends to speak to them.

Accepting their fate, Josh bravely told him: 'I'm so happy with how well we've done. We've got so much to thank *The X Factor* for.'

JJ's voice wobbled as he praised the three finalists, saying: 'We wanna wish the guys the best of luck.'

And Jaymi added: 'I can't describe how amazing it's been. We've loved every moment.'

Louis was nothing but positive about his four boys. 'I'm a little disappointed, but we were ready for it,' he said. 'They're going to have an amazing future. They're going to be the next big boy band!'

You could tell by the tears glistening in his eyes that he truly meant every word.

Before leaving the show, the four-piece gathered for one last song – Taylor Swift's 'Love Story'. Brimming with emotion, their voices soared – it was their *X Factor* swansong and they did themselves proud.

The next day the boys had composed themselves enough to travel to the *Daybreak* studios to chat to Lorraine Kelly – and Rylan Clark, who had been given a job on the top show!

Josh admitted he was gutted to leave the show, but had so many fond memories of his time on *The X Factor*.

'We've had an amazing time – we had the best time of our lives,' he told Lorraine.

Jaymi vowed they would continue to perform as a band and said they were on the lookout for a record deal.

'We're going to take a few days off to be with our family, but we will be back,' the heartthrob promised. 'This is not the end for us at all.'

'I've got to say as well, these boys are four of the nicest and politest boys ever, they've got such a good future,' added their buddy Rylan.

The following week, the boys travelled to Manchester for the live final of the show they had all wanted so much to win. They watched as James Arthur was crowned winner of *The X Factor* 2012, and were overjoyed for him.

The *X Factor* excitement was all over for another year. But for Union J it was the start of a brand new beginning. And with their JCats supporting them, the boys had a bright future ahead of them.

The X Factor 2012 will be remembered for more than just James Arthur's moment of glory – it will be memorable because it introduced Union J and District 3 to the world.

UNION J AND DISTRICT 3: BATTLE OF THE BANDS

And it will definitely be remembered for the epic battle that raged on screen before our very eyes – the battle of the bands...